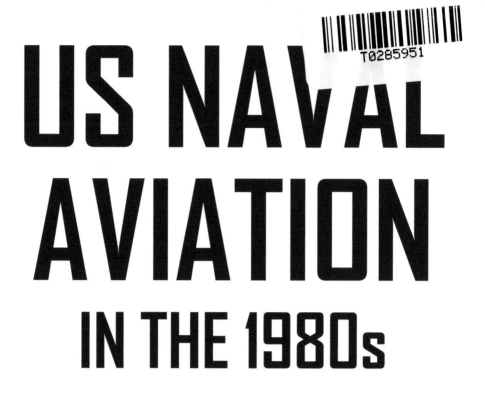

US NAVAL AVIATION

IN THE 1980s

ATLANTIC AND PACIFIC FLEET AIR STATIONS

Adrian Symonds

AMBERLEY

Acknowledgements

I would like to thank Sally Tunnicliffe for her assistance. Special thanks go to my wife, Louise, and son, Charlie.

This book is dedicated to the men and women of U.S. Naval Aviation.

First published 2023

Amberley Publishing
The Hill, Stroud
Gloucestershire, GL5 4EP

www.amberley-books.com

Copyright © Adrian Symonds, 2023

The right of Adrian Symonds to be identified as the Author of this work has been asserted in accordance with the Copyrights, Designs and Patents Act 1988.

ISBN 978 1 4456 9872 4 (print)
ISBN 978 1 4456 9873 1 (ebook)

British Library Cataloguing in Publication Data.
A catalogue record for this book is available from the British Library.

Typesetting by SJmagic DESIGN SERVICES, India.

Contents

Introduction

The United States Navy (USN), already the world's largest, expanded during the 1980s as part of President Reagan's plans for a '600-ship navy', reversing its post-Vietnam decline. The United States Marine Corps (USMC) was the USN's sister service, an expeditionary maritime land force focused on amphibious operations. Although separate services, both were closely integrated and under the Department of the Navy, one of three Department of Defense military departments. Naval Aviation, which celebrated its 75th anniversary in 1986, saw the closest area of USN and USMC integration, largely through the Naval Air Training and Operating Procedures Standardization (NATOPS) programme. NATOPS prescribed harmonised aircraft operation instructions and procedures to all USN and USMC aviation personnel, intended to improve combat readiness and flight safety.

The USN supported three national objectives: prevention of nuclear war through deterrence, by maintaining a ballistic-missile submarine (SSBN) force; defending U.S. and allied territory against major Soviet aggression, by ensuring that the U.S. could move reinforcements and supplies across the Atlantic to the European war zone; and protecting U.S. interests against smaller-scale aggression by the Soviets or by other countries, notably in Third World areas. To fulfil these national objectives, the USN focussed upon sea control, power projection and peacetime presence operations. Naval Aviation directly supported all of these activities.

While the USN's primarily Cold War focus was to contain, and preferably roll back, the Soviet Union and her allies, rising tensions with Iran and several Middle Eastern countries became an increasing preoccupation during the 1980s, drawing Naval Aviation into action.

The Atlantic and Pacific Fleets each controlled two Numbered Fleets. As USN ships and aircraft units deployed from one Numbered Fleet area of responsibility (AOR) to another, they would Change Operational Control (CHOP) to the relevant Numbered Fleet commander.

The Atlantic Fleet (LANTFLT: HQ Norfolk, Virginia) controlled Second Fleet, HQ Norfolk, covering the North Atlantic (NORLANT), and Sixth Fleet, HQ Gaeta, Italy, covering the Mediterranean and Black Seas. LANTFLT also controlled the South Atlantic Force.

The Pacific Fleet (PACFLT: HQ Pearl Harbor, Hawaii) controlled Third Fleet, HQ Pearl Harbor, covering the Central Pacific and Eastern Pacific (EASTPAC), and Seventh Fleet, HQ Yokosuka, Japan, covering the Western Pacific (WESTPAC) and the Indian Ocean (IO).

Additionally there was a Middle East Force and an Indian Ocean Task Force; both LANTFLT and PACFLT ships and aircraft deployed to serve with these forces.

In 1980 the USN and USMC 'total aircraft inventory' (including inactive and stored aircraft) was 6,300: 2,164 combat, 219 transport/utility, seventy-four observation, 884 training, 1,913 miscellaneous and 1,046 rotary wing aircraft. The 1980 'total operating inventory' (total aircraft actually assigned to operational units) was 4,436 aircraft. The total operating inventory remained steady throughout the decade, increasing to 4,534 aircraft in 1982, declining to 4,437 in 1984, before peaking at 4,572 in 1989. Meanwhile, new types and upgraded variants of existing types entered service during the decade, including the AH-1W, AV-8B, CH/MH-53E, E-6A, F/A-18, F-14A+, F-16N and SH-60.

Of the USN's 63,735 officers and 464,265 enlisted personnel in 1980, aviation personnel accounted for 15,395 officers and 98,870 enlisted. Personnel peaked in 1987; 18,552 officers and 110,927 enlisted aviation personnel, out of USN totals of 77,030 officers and 538,675 enlisted. By 1989 aviation accounted for 18,212 officers and 108,496 enlisted, out of a total of 74,913 officers and 540,278 enlisted.

The introduction of surface- and underwater-launched Tomahawk Land Attack Missile (TLAM) cruise missiles, which followed the original Tomahawk Anti-Ship Missile (TASM) into service, gave USN surface ships and submarines the ability to strike inland targets independently of Naval Aviation. TASM entered service in 1983, followed by the nuclear-armed TLAM-N in 1984, the conventional TLAM-C in 1986 and the conventional-submunitions-dispensing TLAM-D in 1988.

Financial pressures from 1986 saw the massive build-up of the U.S. armed forces slow, then reverse; the USN peaked at 594 ships in 1987 while Naval Aviation aircraft strength peaked in 1989. The declining defence budgets from the late 1980s coincided with more restrained U.S rhetoric regarding (and increased engagement with) the Soviet Union, running up to the Cold War's conclusion.

This volume focusses on LANTFLT and PACFLT air stations; a subsequent volume will explore US Marine Corps, Naval Education and Training Command, Naval Air Reserve, and Research, Development and Test air stations.

Arguably the epitome of US Naval Aviation in the 1980s: the F-14 Tomcat. This VF-102 'Diamondbacks' F-14A was assigned to CVW-1, embarked in USS *America* (CV-66). Visible in the background, *America* was conducting an April to November 1984 Mediterranean Sea/Indian Ocean deployment. The Tomcat carries a fleet air defence weapons load. Each wing pylon carries an AIM-7 Sparrow radar-guided, medium-range air-to-air missile (AAM) and an AIM-9 Sidewinder infrared-guided short-range AAM (outboard). On the underside are two AIM-54 Phoenix radar-guided long-range AAMs; to their rear will either be another two AIM-54s or one, centrally mounted, AIM-7. Under each intake trunk is a 267 US Gal (1,011 litre) external fuel tank. (National Archives and Records Administration)

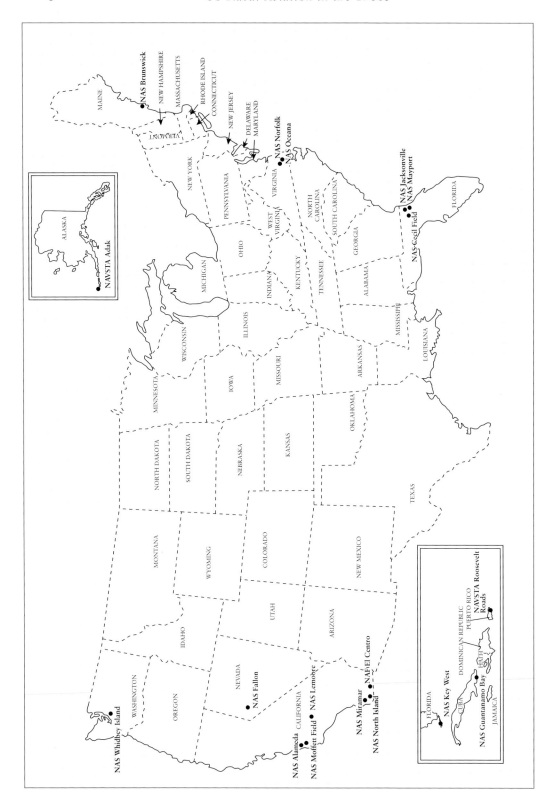

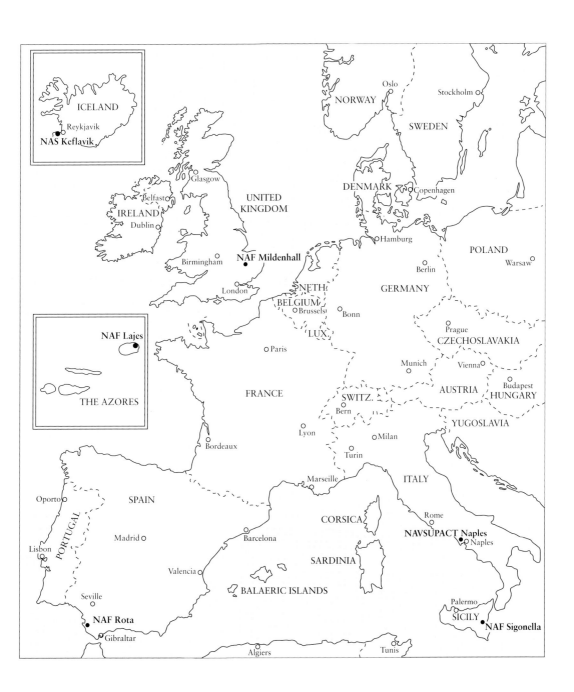

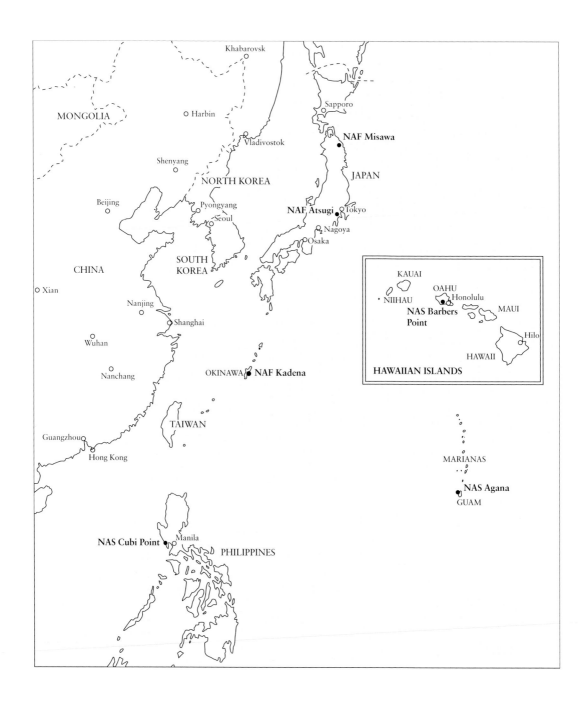

Atlantic Continental Fleet Support Stations

Commander Naval Air Force, U.S. Atlantic Fleet (COMNAVAIRLANT, 'AirLant'), at NAS Norfolk, provided combat-ready aviation forces to Commander-in-Chief, U.S. Atlantic Fleet (CINCLANTFLT). These forces were operationally controlled by the Second and Sixth Fleets (Atlantic and Mediterranean respectively).

In the following description, unit identification letter 'tail codes' are noted in parenthesis after squadron designations, apart from squadrons which were allocated to carrier air wings (CVWs); these squadrons (which periodically switched assigned CVW) took on the CVW's identification letters rather than having their own.

Naval Air Station (NAS) Brunswick, Maine

Brunswick was home to Patrol Squadrons (VP), each with nine P-3s, under Patrol Wing Five (PATWING FIVE), itself (along with PATWING ELEVEN, see p. 15) under Patrol Wings Atlantic (PATWINGSLANT). VP-8 (unit identification: LC) operated P-3Bs, replacing them with P-3C Update IIs during 1981 and P-3C Update II.5s in 1985. VP-10 (LD) replaced its P-3Bs with P-3C Update IIs in 1980. VP-11 (LE) replaced its P-3Bs with P-3C Update II.5s in 1981. VP-23 (LJ), VP-26 (LK) and VP-44 (LM) had operated P-3C Update IIs since 1978/79.

A P-3C Orion of NAS Brunswick's VP-8 'Tigers', operating from Albrook Air Force Station, in the Panama Canal Zone, during Exercise UNITAS XXV in 1984. The UNITAS exercises between the United States and South American navies commenced in 1959. UNITAS XXV was the naval exercise's silver anniversary; it lasted 129 days, 77 of them involving bilateral/multilateral exercises. Fifty ships and over 100 aircraft from Brazil, Chile, Colombia, Peru, Uruguay, Venezuela and the United States took part. UNITAS XXV also included six amphibious operations, special warfare and aviation cross training, and coast guard symposia. (NARA)

The Naval Security Group Activities – Special Program Group (NAVSECGRUACT SPEC. PROG. GP.), was established on 1 July 1982 under the Naval Security Group, assigned to PATWING FIVE. This was engaged in secretive 'special projects' duties and was assigned a pair of P-3Bs. This unit became VPU-1 (VPU – Patrol Squadron Special Projects Unit) from 1985, adding a third P-3B in 1985 and replacing one P-3B with a P-3A from 1986. By 1988 VPU-1 operated two P-3Cs, one UP-3 and one P-3A, relinquishing the latter in 1989. VPU-1 P-3s routinely wore markings of fleet P-3 squadrons, complete with Bureau Numbers (BuNos) of P-3Cs (and sometimes other types) with false 'windows' and 'sonobouy tubes' painted on.

A revolutionary new type of reserve unit was established aboard Brunswick on 13 January 1984, the Patrol Squadron Master Augment Unit, VP-MAU (identification code LB). While existing reserve VP units operated older P-3 models, VP-MAU was equipped with brand new P-3C Update IIs. Unlike those reserve VP units, VP-MAU was not intended to operate as a complete squadron; if mobilised, its maintenance and flight crews were to be absorbed into the regular VP units. When a second VP-MAU ('VP-MAU Moffett') was established at Moffett Field on 20 December 1986, the original VP-MAU at Brunswick was redesignated 'VP-MAU Brunswick'. To its pair of P-3C Update IIs, three P-3As were added from 1986; an EP-3A was also assigned during 1987.

Brunswick's station flight (7F) operated one C-1A (replaced by a UC-12B during 1980) and two (from 1982, one) UH-1Ns.

NAS Cecil Field, Florida

Sea Based Anti-Submarine Warfare Wings Atlantic (SEABASEDASWWINGSLANT) at Jacksonville controlled Cecil Field's Air Anti-Submarine Wing One (CVSW ONE), redesignated Sea-Strike Wing One (SSW ONE) in 1988, which administratively controlled Cecil Field's S-3-equipped Air Anti-Submarine Squadrons (VS).

Also at Cecil were the A-7 Attack Squadrons (VA) and later F/A-18 Strike Fighter Squadrons (VFA – designated Fighter Attack Squadrons until 25 March 1983) under Light Attack Wing One (LATWING ONE), which in turn was under Tactical Wings Atlantic (TACWINGSLANT) at Oceana.

Strike Fighter Wings Atlantic (STRKFIGHTWINGSLANT) was established at Cecil on 1 October 1986, subsequently controlling Cecil Field's active units, not only the VA/VFA units of LATWING ONE, but also the CVSW ONE/SSW ONE VS units. Cecil's deployable VA/VFA/VS units were operationally assigned to CVWs for sea deployments. STRKFIGHTWINGSLANT continued to report to TACWINGSLANT.

CVSW ONE/SSW ONE controlled VSSU (the Air ASW Support Unit) (AR), AirLant's S-3A replacement aircrew and maintenance personnel training unit. In January 1987 VS-27 (AD) was established to take over as AirLant's S-3 training 'Fleet Replacement Squadron' (FRS), equipped with S-3Bs (the first squadron to receive the improved variant). Deployable units were VS-22, VS-24, VS-28, VS-30, VS-31 and VS-32, each usually with around ten S-3As. In July 1988 VS-30 became the first fleet operational squadron to receive S-3Bs.

Permanent squadrons (as opposed to operationally deployable ones) under LATWING ONE were VA-174, VA-45 and VFA-106. VA-174 (AD), AirLant's A-7 FRS, had a large A-7E/TA-7C fleet, respectively operating thirty-seven/twenty-two in 1980–81, with

Two VS-24 'Scouts' S-3A Vikings seen during 1986. VS-24 was assigned to CVW-8/USS *Nimitz* (CVN-68). The furthest S-3 displays the original carrier aircraft scheme: FS16440 Light Gull Gray topsides and gloss FS17875 Insignia White undersides. The nearest S-3 is in the replacement, toned-down, Tactical Paint Scheme (TPS) introduced during the 1980s. TPS application varied between aircraft types; the S-3 version of TPS consisted of overall FS 36375 Light Ghost Gray with FS 35237 Blue Gray around the cockpit. (NARA)

A VS-30 'Diamond Cutters' S-3A at NAS Fallon during 1985. It carries Mk 76 Mod 5, 25-pound, practice bombs on the underwing TER. When S-3 squadrons participated in full-CVW integration Strike Det deployments to Fallon, they obviously could not practice their ASW role in Nevada, but they conducted conventional bombing training instead. VS-30 was assigned to CVW-17/USS *Saratoga* (CV-60). (NARA)

Seen at Fallon for Strike Det during 1988, this VS-32 'Maulers' S-3A features toned-down markings while retaining the Light Gull Gray/Insignia White scheme. It carries live 500-pound Mk 82 Snakeye retarded bombs on its TER. (NARA)

numbers reducing (twenty-one/eleven were operated by 1987) as the A-7 was supplanted by F/A-18s. VA-174 also operated a single T-39D until 1980. VA-174 disestablished on 30 June 1988. VA-45 (AD) was an adversary squadron with twelve TA-4Js; it relocated to Key West during 1980 (q.v.). VFA-106 (AD) was established on 27 April 1984 as AirLant's F/A-18 FRS, building up to forty-three F/A-18A/Bs by 1986. Three T-34Cs joined VFA-106 from 1988, providing Forward Air Control (Airborne) (FAC(A)) services for F/A-18 students over weapons ranges during the air-to-ground syllabus.

In 1980 LATWING ONE's deployable units were VA-12, VA-15, VA-37, VA-46, VA-66, VA-72, VA-81, VA-82, VA-83, VA-86, VA-87 and VA-105, each with around twelve A-7Es. As F/A-18As replaced A-7Es, new VFA squadrons were established to accommodate F/A-18As, while VA squadrons were gradually disestablished, or re-equipped with F/A-18s and redesignated as VFAs. VFA-131 and VFA-132 arrived at Cecil with F/A-18As during 1985, after training under VFA-125 at Lemoore (q.v.). During 1986 VA-12 and VA-66 were disestablished, while VA-15 and VA-87 were redesignated VFA-15 and VFA-87; newly established VFA-136 and VFA-137 also arrived at Cecil; all with F/A-18As. During 1987 VA-82/VA-86 became VFA-82/VFA-86 with improved F/A-18Cs, VFA-82 being the first fleet F/A-18C squadron. During 1988 VA-81/VA-83 became VFA-81/VFA-83 with F/A-18Cs. VA-37, VA-46, VA-72 and VA-105 still retained A-7Es at decade's end.

A VA-174 'Hellrazors' TA-7C transiting through NAS Dallas in February 1988, shortly before AirLant's A-7 FRS disestablished. (NARA)

A VFA-106 'Gladiators' F/A-18B seen during 1987. A proportion of VFA-106's Hornets, including this example, carried 'MARINES' rather than 'NAVY' titles, reflecting the fact that this FRS also trained USMC personnel. (NARA)

Two A-7E Corsair IIs of VA-72 'Blue Hawks' during 1982 while assigned to CVW-1, embarked in USS *America* during the latter's December 1982 to June 1983 Mediterranean Sea and Indian Ocean deployment. Both aircraft carry empty TERs (triple ejector racks for bombs). While the nearest aircraft carries an underwing external fuel tank on station 6, the furthest aircraft carries an AN/AAR-45 forward-looking infrared (FLIR) pod on station 6. Only station 6 was wired for AN/AAR-45. When carrying the FLIR pod, no self-defence AIM-9 would be mounted on station 5 (the starboard cheek station) as to fire a Sidewinder from station 5 with AN/AAR-45 fitted to station 6 may damage the latter. Consequently, no AIM-9 rail is fitted to station 5 on the furthest aircraft. These A-7Es are in the original Light Gull Gray/Insignia White scheme with full colour markings. (NARA)

A TPS-camouflaged VA-86 'Sidewinders' A-7E deployed to NAS Fallon during 1986. The A-7E TPS variant consisted of FS 36320 Dark Ghost Gray upper surfaces/sides and FS 36375 Light Ghost Gray under surfaces. Initially markings were to be in the 'opposite' shade of grey, as seen here. While this example is pristine, in service, especially when deployed at sea, the scheme quickly deteriorated with the greys fading into each other, making markings almost impossible to decipher. This was compounded when squadrons applied any available grey/light blue shade to touch up aircraft during corrosion work, resulting in an even more blotchy appearance. Therefore, regulations were amended to allow MODEX numbers to be in very dark grey, or black as seen here; later all markings were similarly darkened. This A-7E carries an AN/AAR-45 FLIR pod; the outboard pylon is fitted with an empty TER. The 'E' behind the cockpit denotes that VA-86 had been awarded the Battle Effectiveness Award (known as Battle 'E'), awarded to a small number of USN ships, submarines and aviation squadrons each year. VA-86 was assigned to CVW-8/USS *Nimitz*. (NARA)

This VFA-137 'Kestrels' F/A-18A Hornet is also seen while deployed to NAS Fallon during 1987. The F/A-18 was the first type to feature TPS from the outset, The F/A-18 TPS version initially consisted of FS 36375 Light Ghost Gray topsides, FS 36495 Light Gray undersides/radome and FS 35237 Blue Gray on the area from in front of the cockpit to the cannons. This F/A-18A carries an Airborne Instrumentation Subsystem (AIS) pod for the Air Combat Maneuvering Instrumentation (ACMI)/Tactical Air Combat Training System (TACTS) on the wingtip; when used over an instrumented range, this allowed training aerial engagements to be tracked for subsequent review and debrief. VFA-137 was assigned to CVW-13/USS *Coral Sea* (CV-43). (NARA)

Two F/A-18Cs of VFA-86 'Sidewinders' over Townsend Bombing Range in Georgia during 1989. VFA-86 was assigned to CVW-1 aboard USS *America*. The F/A-18C (and D) introduced a simplified two-tone version of TPS compared to F/A-18A/B models: FS 36320 Dark Ghost Gray topsides and FS 36375 Light Ghost Gray undersides. Improved F/A-18C/D variants could be externally differentiated from original F/A-18A/B variants by the addition on the C/D of two blisters behind the cockpit and an additional fairing on the rear of the fin tops. These additions relate to the AN/ALQ-165 Advanced Self-Protection Jammer; this internal ECM jammer system was later dropped by the USN for use on F/A-18C/Ds (although it was reintroduced much later on the F/A-18E/F Super Hornet). (NARA)

Reserve units at Cecil were Naval Air Reserve VA-203 with A-7Bs (A-7Es from 1985) and Marine Air Reserve, Marine Attack Squadron VMA-142 (MB) with A-4Fs/ TA-4Js (A-4M/TA-4F from 1988), under Marine Aircraft Group 42 Detachment A (MAG-42 Det A).

Cecil's station flight (7U) operated a single C-1A (two during 1984-85) until 1986; a C-12 was operated from 1988.

NAS Jacksonville, Florida

Jacksonville was home to PATWING ELEVEN's VPs and the Helicopter Anti-Submarine Squadrons (HS) of Helicopter Anti-Submarine Wing One (HELASWING ONE). PATWING ELEVEN controlled VP-5 (LA), VP-16 (LF), VP-24 (LR), VP-45 (LN), VP-49 (LP) and VP-56 (LQ), each with nine P-3Cs. HELASWING ONE controlled HS-3, HS-5, HS-7, HS-9, HS-11 and HS-15 each with six SH-3s. HS-5 and HS-11 operated SH-3Ds until replacing them with SH-3Hs from 1983; the others used SH-3Hs throughout. Single SH-3Gs were allocated to HS-9 during early 1983 and HS-5 during late 1983 to early 1984. HS-17 was established 4 April 1984, operating a mixed SH-3D/H fleet.

A VP-5 'Mad Foxes' P-3C seen during 1988. It carries an AGM-84 Harpoon anti-ship missile underwing. P-3s (along with several other large land-based naval types) utilised a colour scheme which reversed that used by carrier aircraft, featuring Insignia White topsides and Light Gull Gray undersides; the white topsides were intended to reflect solar heat from the top of the fuselage. (NARA)

An SH-3H Sea King of HS-3 'Tridents', assigned to CVW-17, lands aboard its carrier, USS *Saratoga*, during 1986. Unlike fixed-wing carrier aircraft, SH-3s featured Insignia White topsides and Light Gull Gray undersides, until they too switched to TPS. (NARA)

An SH-3H of HS-5 'Nightdippers', assigned to CVW-7 aboard USS *Dwight D. Eisenhower* (CVN-69), seen in the background, during the latter's February to August 1988 Mediterranean cruise. This SH-3H has adopted the helicopter variant of TPS, which consisted of FS 36375 Light Ghost Gray fuselage sides, FS 35237 Blue Gray on upward facing surfaces and FS 36495 Light Gray undersides. (NARA)

Jacksonville housed the east-coast P-3 and SH-3 FRS training squadrons. VP-30 (LL), directly under PATWINGSLANT, operated various TP-/VP-3As, P-3A/B/Cs. HS-1 (AR), under HELASWING ONE, operated SH-3D/G/Hs. HS-1 also maintained two overseas detachments: Det 1 operated a utility-configured SH-3G supporting Commander, Middle Eastern Force (COMMIDEASTFOR) on USS *La Salle* (AGF-3) and at Manama, Bahrain. Det 2 operated a VIP-configured SH-3G supporting Commander, U.S. Sixth Fleet at Gaeta, Italy, and aboard his flagship: USS *Puget Sound* (AD-38) from 1980, USS *Coronado* (AGF-11) from 1985 and USS *Belknap* (CG-26) from 1986. HS-1's dets were taken over by HC-2 (q.v.) upon its 1 April 1987 establishment.

In early 1980 the station flight (7E) was assigned a US-2B, a UC-12B and four HH-46As; from later that year it operated a UC-12B and up to three SH-3Ds.

Reserve squadrons were Fleet Logistics Support Squadron VR-58 (JV – three C-9Bs) and VP-62 (LT – nine P-3Bs); during 1985 reserve HS-75 (six SH-3Ds) moved to Jacksonville from NAS Willow Grove, Pennsylvania. From 5 December 1987, VP-62 became the first Reserve squadron to transition to P-3C Update IIIs, completing re-equipment on 31 March 1989.

Jacksonville housed a major aircraft overhaul facility, Naval Air Rework Facility (NARF) Jacksonville, renamed Naval Aviation Depot (NADEP) Jacksonville in 1987; it was primarily concerned with A-4, A-7 and F/A-18 major overhauls.

A C-9B Skytrain II of VR-58 'Sunseekers' landing at NAS Oceana during 1989. (NARA)

An SH-3D of HS-75 'Emerald Knights' during 1985.
(NARA)

NAS Key West, Florida

Aboard Key West was a detachment of Fighter Squadron VF-171 (AirLant's Oceana-based F-4 FRS – q.v.). VF-171 Det Key West (AD) operated between six and ten F-4Ns, replaced by around seven F-4Ss in 1983. The Det also operated two or three A-4Es and a TA-4J in the adversary role. VF-171 Det Key West decommissioned on 30 April 1984, ahead of the parent squadron's disestablishment on 1 June 1984.

VF-101, the F-14 FRS at Oceana (q.v.), had periodically sent short detachments to Key West, but on 27 June 1989 a permanent VF-101 Det Key West (AD) was formed at Key West with ten F-14As.

As noted, adversary squadron VA-45 (AD) transferred from Cecil Field during 1980 with its ten TA-4Js, adding a T-39 that year. VF-171 Det Key West's three A-4Es and TA-4J were transferred to VA-45 in February to March 1984. On 7 February 1985 VA-45 was redesignated VF-45 and reassigned from TACWINGSLANT to Fighter Wing One (FITWING ONE). By 1987 VF-45 operated seven A-4Es, five TA-4Js and a T-39. In October 1987 new F-16N/TF-16Ns (ten/two) joined VF-45, considerably increasing its ability to replicate modern threats; in 1989 VF-45 transferred six of its F-16Ns and a TF-16N to Oceana's VF-43. Late in 1989, VF-45 started to receive ex-US Air Force (USAF) F-5Es and an ex-TOPGUN F-5F.

VAQ-33 primarily provided electronic warfare (EW) aggressors, conducting stand-off jamming, chaff laying, missile simulation and communications jamming/deception for

Above left: A TA-4J Skyhawk of VF-45 'Blackbirds' visiting NAS Dallas during 1988. It displays one of many adversary schemes used by the squadron. (NARA)

Above right: A VF-45 F-16N Fighting Falcon taking off from NAS Oceana during 1989. It wears the standard three-tone 'Aegean' scheme that F-16N/TF-16Ns were delivered in: FS 36307 Light Sea Gray, FS 36251 Aggressor Gray and FS 35237 Medium Blue Gray. Incidentally, this was the same scheme applied to F-16C/Ds exported to Greece. (NARA)

exercises. VAQ was the abbreviation for 'Carrier Special Squadron, Tactical Electronics', redesignated 'Tactical Electronic Warfare Squadron' from 1987. VAQ-33 (GD) operated a diverse fleet: single examples of NC-121K (the final Constellation in US military service, retired on 11 June 1982), P-3A (from 1983, replacing the NC-121K) and EP-3A (from 1987), and varying numbers of EF-4J (until 1981), TA-3B, ERA-3B, KA-3B (from 1985), EA-4F (until 1988), TA-4J (from 1981 until 1988), EA-6A and TA-7C (from 1988). VAQ-33 also acted as the sole A-3 FRS; these training responsibilities were the main preoccupation of the squadron's five TA-3Bs, although they were sometimes used as targets during exercises. VAQ-33 was under TACWINGSLANT administrative control until 1981, subsequently under Tactical Support Wing One (TACSUPWING ONE). Operational control came from the Fleet Electronic Warfare Support Group (FEWSG).

Key West's station flight operated three SH-3Gs, replaced by SH-3Ds in 1981, plus a US-2B until 1980; a C-12 was assigned from 1981.

NAVSTA/NAF/NAS Mayport, Florida

Naval Station (NAVSTA) Mayport, the air side of which became Naval Air Facility (NAF) Mayport in 1983 and NAS Mayport in 1988, was home to LAMPS (Light

Above: ERA-3B Skywarrior, BuNo 144827/'GD-101' of VAQ-33 'Firebirds', seen on 8 November 1987, deployed to Elmendorf Air Force Base, Alaska, during the Third Fleet North Pacific Exercise (NORPACEX). On 16 November, while returning to Elmendorf following a NORPACEX mission, this aircraft collided with VAQ-33's KA-3B 138925/'GD 140' and crashed into the Pacific; two of its four crew members were recovered injured, the body of one was later recovered and the forth was not found. The KA-3B managed to return to Elmendorf despite losing its port engine. (NARA)

Left: A VAQ-33 KA-3B refuelling a VC-12 TA-4J during 1980. (NARA)

An SH-60B Seahawk of HSL-44 'Swamp
Foxes' over NAS Mayport during 1989.
SH-60Bs were delivered from the outset in
TPS. (NARA)

Airborne Multi-Purpose System) helicopters. LAMPS helicopters, primarily intended
to deploy individually or in pairs to operate from USN frigates, destroyers and cruisers,
performed anti-submarine warfare (ASW), anti-ship surveillance and targeting (ASST),
as well as search and rescue (SAR). SH-2F LAMPS Mk Is were joined by much improved
SH-60B LAMPS Mk IIIs during the decade. SH-2Fs were retained in service after the
SH-60B's introduction, as the USN's Knox-class frigates, and most early Oliver Hazard
Perry-class frigates did not have the required equipment to operate SH-60Bs.

HSL-36 (HY) (HSL: Helicopter Anti-Submarine Squadron, Light) operated
SH-2Fs under Helicopter Sea Control Wing One (HELSEACONWING ONE).
HELSEACONWING THREE was later established to control the new SH-60B
squadrons: HSL-42 (HN), established 5 Oct 1984; HSL-40 (HK), established 4 Oct
1985 (as AirLant's FRS); HSL-44 (HP), established 21 Aug 1986; HSL-46 (HQ),
established 7 Apr 1988; and HSL-48 (HR), established 7 Sep 1989. Each squadron
operated around ten SH-60Bs.

The base flight (8U) operated two U-11As until 1982; a UC-12B was assigned from 1988.

NAS Norfolk, Virginia

Norfolk accommodated Carrier Airborne Early Warning Wing Twelve (CAEWW-12),
with Carrier Airborne Early Warning Squadrons (VAWs) usually assigned four E-2Cs
each. Deployable squadrons VAW-121, VAW-122, VAW-123, VAW-124, VAW-125 and
VAW-126 were joined by VAW-127, established on 2 September 1983. RVAW-120
(RVAW-Carrier Airborne Early Warning Training Squadron, redesignated VAW-120 on
1 May 1983) (AD) was AirLant's FRS, operating around six E-2Cs and two TE-2Cs.
The C-2A carrier on-board delivery (COD) aircraft was an E-2 development. Seventeen
were built in the 1960s; by the 1980s they served alongside larger numbers of even older
radial engine-powered C-1As. Therefore the C-2A was placed back into production.
Thirty-nine were ordered in 1984 to first replace the C-1As and then the original C-2As;
new production aircraft were designated C-2A(R), 'R' for 'Re-procured'. Consequently
VAW-120 also gained C-2A training responsibilities, receiving the USN's first C-2A(R)
in June 1985, and subsequently having two or three assigned.

An E-2C Hawkeye of
VAW-124 'Bear Aces',
which was assigned to
CVW-8/USS *Theodore
Roosevelt* (CVN-71),
seen on Strike Det
deployment to Fallon
during 1988. (NARA)

A VAW-120 C-2A
Greyhound visiting
NAS Oceana during
1989. (NARA)

Also at Norfolk were HELSEACONWING ONE helicopter squadrons. Deployable
HSL squadrons HSL-32 (HV) and HSL-34 (HX), each operated around ten SH-2Fs;
HSL-30 (HT) was AirLant's FRS with around ten SH-2Fs (and a HH-2D until 1984).
Helicopter Mine Countermeasures Squadrons HM-14 (BJ) and HM-16 (GC) each
initially operated eight RH-53Ds mine countermeasures (MCM) helicopters, subsequently
with between five and seven per squadron. HM-16 disestablished on 2 January 1987.
Thereafter HM-14's fleet increased, peaking at eleven RH-53Ds in 1988; it began
replacing its RH-53Ds with MH-53Es in 1989. HM-15 (TB) established at Norfolk
on 2 January 1987, with four MH-53Es, moving to Alameda, California/AirPac, on
1 October 1987. HM-12 (DH) was AirLant's CH/RH-53 FRS with five RH-53Ds, adding
CH-53Es during 1983. As well as training, HM-12 also provided fleet logistics vertical
on-board delivery (VOD) support to the east coast and throughout the Caribbean. In
1987 HM-12 transferred its CH-53E VOD duties to newly established HC-2. On 28 May
1987 HM-12 received its first MH-53E, the improved MCM variant, and operated two
CH-53Es and five MH-53Es by 1989. HM-12/-14/-16 were later reassigned to Helicopter
Tactical Wing One (HELTACWING ONE), which was established on 1 October 1982.
    Norfolk units under TACSUPWING ONE included Helicopter Combat Support
Squadron HC-6 (HW) and Fleet Logistics Support Squadron VRC-40 (JK). Vertical
replenishment (VERTREP) was the primary mission for HC-6's twenty-three CH-46Ds in
1980, along with SAR. Subsequently, HC-6 operated a mixed CH/HH/UH-46A and CH/
HH/UH-46D fleet. HC-6 also had a LANTFLT VIP det with four VH-3As, until 1987 when
HC-2 absorbed this responsibility. From 1985 HC-6 was reassigned to HELTACWING
ONE. VRC-40 conducted COD with C-1As, transitioning to C-2As in 1986, also operating
a pair of CT-39Es, reducing to one in 1989. On 1 October 1986, TACSUPWING ONE's
VRF-31, the USN's last aircraft ferry squadron, was disestablished at Norfolk.

An SH-2F Sea Sprite of HSL-30 'Scooters' landing aboard the Spruance-class destroyer USS *Nicholson* (DD-982) during 1983. This SH-2F is in overall FS 16081 Engine Gray, the standard USN scheme for helicopters (apart from SH-3s) until TPS was adopted. (NARA)

This is the same HSL-30 SH-2F, BuNo 149026/'HT-030', seen in the previous image, but by the time of this 1986 photograph it had been repainted in toned-down TPS. (NARA)

Right: An HM-12 'Sea Dragons' RH-53D Sea Stallion flying over the Norfolk area during 1984; it is finished in the standard overall Engine Gray scheme. (NARA)

Below: A VRC-40 'Rawhides' C-1A Trader is directed by the yellow shirt flight deck chief aboard USS *John F. Kennedy* (CV-67) during 1984. (NARA)

Also aboard Norfolk under TACSUPWING ONE was Fleet Composite Squadron VC-6 (JG). It did not operate manned aircraft, but seaborne and airborne targets, later adding Pioneer RPVs (remotely piloted vehicles). While 'VC-6 Shore' was at Norfolk, its assets were detached. VC-6 Det Dam Neck, located at Fleet Combat Training Center Atlantic, Dam Neck, Virginia, operated aerial targets: MQM-74C until 1984 and BQM-34S from 1982. VC-6 Sea Det component at Naval Amphibious Base, Little Creek, Virginia, operated QST-33 and QST-35 SEPTAR (Seaborne Powered Target) surface targets. VC-6 was assigned the USN's Remotely Piloted Vehicle (RPV) Program in 1984, later renamed the Unmanned Air Vehicle (UAV) Program. This included both the 'Short Range RPV surveillance program' and the Mid-Range Reconnaissance BQM-74C; for the latter Northrop provided ten BQM-74C tactical reconnaissance variants for evaluation, although this variant did not proceed into production. The Pioneer RPV was selected to fulfil the short range RPV role, conducting gunnery spotting from Iowa-class battleships. VC-6 RPV Det 1 was established at NAS Patuxent River, Maryland, in July 1986 to operate Pioneer, primarily from Iowa-class battleships.

HC-8 (BR) was established under HELTACWING ONE on 3 December 1984; by late 1985 it had built up to thirteen H-46s, with a mixed CH-46A/HH-46A/CH-46D/ UH-46D fleet, standardising on HH-46D/CH-46D/UH-46D models by 1988.

One of VC-6 'Skeet of the Fleet' Sea Det's QST-35 SEPTAR target boats in use during a Harpoon anti-ship missile test from the guided missile cruiser USS *Ticonderoga* (CG-47) near the Atlantic Fleet Weapons Training Facility, Roosevelt Roads, Puerto Rico, during 1983. (NARA)

A UH-46D Sea Knight of HC-8 'Dragon Whales', assigned to the Mars-class combat stores ship USS *Sylvania* (AFS-2), plying its trade during 1988. Like most other USN helicopters, it is finished in overall Engine Gray. (NARA)

HC-2 (HU) was established under HELTACWING ONE on 1 April 1987, absorbing components from several squadrons. HC-2 took over HC-6's former LANTFLT VIP det and its four VH-3As, and HM-12's former VOD det and its two CH-53Es. HS-2 also absorbed HS-1 Det 1's utility-configured SH-3G supporting COMMIDEASTFOR in Bahrain (as 'HC-2 Det 2'), and HS-1 Det 2's VIP-configured SH-3G supporting Commander, U.S. Sixth Fleet at Gaeta, Italy, and aboard his flagship USS *Belknap* (as 'HC-2 Det 1'). By 1989, HC-2 operated four VH-3As, two CH-53Es and seven SH-3Gs aboard Norfolk, plus the Italy and Bahrain SH-3G detachments.

Norfolk's station flight (7C) operated two C-131Fs and two UC-12Bs, adding a third UC-12B in 1983. The C-131Fs were retired in 1986. From 1988 it operated two UC-12Bs and two UC-12Ms.

Several Naval Air Reserve squadrons were stationed aboard Norfolk. VAW-78 operated E-2Bs (E-2Cs from 1984). VR-56 (JU) operated three C-9Bs. Helicopter Light Attack Squadron HAL-4 (NW) operated eight HH-1Ks, supporting Naval Special Warfare (NSW) and Explosive Ordnance Disposal (EOD) teams. On 1 October 1989, HAL-4 was redesignated Helicopter Combat Support Special Squadron HCS-4 (NW), re-equipped with HH-60Hs and added Strike Rescue (Combat SAR) to its primary NSW/EOD support mission. VAQ-209 operated EA-6As. HM-18 (NW) was established on 1 October 1986 with RH-53Ds. Marine Medium Helicopter Squadron HMM-774 (MQ) operated eight CH-46Ds, replaced by fourteen CH-46Es from 1984. HMM-774 was under MAG-46 Det A. MAG-46 (HQ: Marine Corps Air Station – MCAS – El Toro, California) was in turn under 4th Marine Aircraft Wing (MAW)/ Marine Air Reserve. NARU (Naval Air Reserve Unit) Norfolk (6S) operated a C-131F until 1980.

Right: U.S. Navy SEAL team members rappel from a HAL-4 'Red Wolves' HH-1K Iroquois while conducting Naval Special Warfare training during 1987. (NARA)

Below: A VAQ-209 'Star Warriors' EA-6A Intruder landing aboard USS *Dwight D. Eisenhower* during CVWR-20's June–July 1984 WESTLANT deployment on 'Ike'. (NARA)

The Fleet Electronic Warfare
Support Group (FEWSG) EC-24A
during 1988. (clipperarctic)

Also aboard Norfolk was FEWSG (Fleet Electronic Warfare Support Group). FEWSG provided EW aggressors for exercises, operationally controlling VAQ-33 at Key West (q.v.). As demand upon VAQ-33 increased, a new dedicated AirPac FEWSG squadron, VAQ-34, was established on 1 March 1983 at NAS Point Mugu, California. Under direct FEWSG control were two NKC-135As modified for EW aggressor duties (periodically updated and further modified), operated and maintained under contract by McDonnel Douglas from Tulsa International Airport, Oklahoma. In 1987 these were joined by an EC-24A (converted DC-8-54F) in the same role. In late 1989 Chrysler Technologies Airborne Systems took over the contract and moved the NKC-135As and EC-24A to Waco Airport, Texas. FEWSG also directly controlled two 'surface detachments', Det 1 at Norfolk, and Det 2 at North Island, operating ULQ-13 EW simulation vans, which could be deployed ashore or at sea.

NARF Norfolk (NADEP Norfolk from 1987) was primarily concerned with A-6 and F-14 major overhauls.

NAS Oceana, Virginia

Aboard Oceana was FITWING ONE and Medium Attack Wing One (MATWING ONE); their deployable squadrons were operationally assigned to CVWs.

Half of FITWING ONE's deployable Fighter Squadrons (each with around twelve aircraft) still operated F-4Js in 1980: VF-11 (transitioning to F-14As in October 1980), VF-31 (F-14A from January 1981), VF-33 (F-14A from late 1981), VF-74 (F-4S from February 1982 then F-14A from February 1983), VF-102 (F-14As from June 1981) and VF-103 (F-4S from 1981 then F-14A from January 1983). The remaining deployable Fighter Squadrons already operated F-14As in 1980: VF-14, VF-32, VF-41, VF-84, VF-142 and VF-143. During 1989, VF-142 and VF-143 transitioned to the improved and re-engined F-14A+. To replace the RF-8G reconnaissance detachments on carriers, one of the two F-14 squadrons in each supercarrier CVW had three of its assigned F-14As wired to carry the Tactical Airborne Reconnaissance Pod System (TARPS). TARPS squadrons were VF-31, VF-32, VF-84, VF-102, VF-103 and VF-143. Originally intended as an interim reconnaissance capability, pending a reconnaissance F/A-18 variant, the latter never materialised in fleet service and therefore TARPS became an ongoing solution.

FITWING ONE also controlled several permanent squadrons. VF-43 was an adversary squadron with a mixed F-5E, T-38A (until 1985), A-4E/F and TA-4J fleet. Due to concerns about spin recovery in the F-14, VF-43 added three T-2Cs in 1980 for F-14 pilot spin recovery training. It added twelve F-21As (leased from Israel) from April 1985, losing its F-5Es soon thereafter; the F-21As were returned to Israel in March 1988. In 1989 VF-43 received six F-16Ns and a TF-16N from VF-45; F-5E/Fs also rejoined VF-43 soon thereafter. The A-4E/Fs and TA-4Js were retained throughout. VF-101 (AD) was AirLant's F-14 FRS, operating a large F-14A fleet (peaking at thirty-six aircraft); on 11 April 1988 VF-101 received the first F-14A+

A VF-102 'Diamondbacks' F-14A. VF-102 joined CVW-1 in 1982, assigned to USS *America*, after replacing its F-4Js with F-14As; this F-14A is seen during VF-102's first deployment aboard *America*, to the South Atlantic May to July 1982. A live AIM-9L is visible underwing. Development of TPS started in 1976; however, this would take several years to develop and evaluate before it could replace the Light Gull Gray/Insignia White scheme. Therefore, on 18 February 1977 a temporary scheme was authorised for carrier-based F-4s and F-14s, eliminating the highly visible Insignia White undersides. The overall Light Gull Gray scheme seen here, retaining full-colour markings, was the result, most F-4s and F-14s receiving this temporary scheme by 1980. (NARA)

A VF-33 'Starfighters' F-14A seen during the same 1982 South Atlantic, USS *America*, deployment as the previous image. VF-33 had also just joined CVW-1, assigned to *America*, also having just replaced its F-4Js with F-14As. Visible underwing are an AIM-7F and an AIM-9L, both live; the forward AIM-54 pallet is empty. This early F-14A only features the small fairing under the chin for the ALQ-100 ECM antenna. Soon an AN/ALR-23 Infrared Search and Track (IRST) pod (in various configurations, with or without underslung ECM antenna) was introduced. From 1983 this was replaced by the definitive AXX-1 Television Camera System (TCS), with underslung ECM antenna. This F-14A is in the colourful marking of aircraft assigned to the squadron commanding officer (CO); CO's aircraft also usually featured an 'x01' MODEX. (NARA)

An F-14A of VF-143 'World Famous Pukin' Dogs', assigned to CVW-7 aboard USS *Dwight D. Eisenhower*, launches from Ike's No. 4 waist catapult during that carrier's February to August 1988 Mediterranean cruise. Visible under the chin is the AXX-1 Television Camera System (TCS); this allowed the crew to visually identify targets at long range. This F-14A is specially marked as the 'CAG bird', the aircraft of the Commander, Carrier Air Wing (COMCVW), who was colloquially known by the obsolete term 'CAG' – for Commander, Air Group. The CAG bird featured an 'x00' MODEX. (NARA)

assigned to an operational squadron. Three spin recovery training T-2Cs were briefly assigned during 1981. As previously noted, on 27 June 1989 a permanent VF-101 Det Key West was formed; temporary detachments had been made to Key West prior to that. VF-171 (AD) was AirLant's F-4 FRS, transitioning from F-4Js to F-4Ss between 1981 and 1983. As noted, it also maintained VF-171 Det Key West with F-4s/A-4s. VF-171 disestablished on 1 June 1984, passing responsibility for training the final USN F-4 crews to the USMC's VMFAT-101 at MCAS Yuma, Arizona.

A VF-43 'Challengers' A-4E taking off from Oceana during 1989. VF-43's mixed fleet standardised on the 'Aegean' camouflage scheme seen here. An AIS pod is barely visible under the starboard wing. (NARA)

A VF-43 T-2C Buckeye also taking off from Oceana during 1989. While VF-43's T-2Cs primarily provided spin recovery refresher training for F-14 crews, they were occasionally also used for air combat manoeuvring (ACM) training, demonstrating light attack/trainer jet characteristics. Consequently, VF-43 camouflaged its T-2Cs; over on the West Coast, VF-126, which also operated T-2C spin trainers, retained the standard Training Command white/orange scheme on their T-2Cs. (NARA)

A VF-43 F-21A Kfir seen at Fallon during 1986. Note the AIS pod under the wing. (NARA)

An F-4S of VF-171 'Aces', AirLant's F-4 FRS, seen conducting training aboard USS *America* during 1984. The tail of a VA-42 A-6 is visible to the left. (NARA)

MATWING ONE was assigned VA-34, VA-35, VA-65, VA-75, VA-85 and VA-176, each generally with ten A-6Es and four KA-6Ds, and operationally assigned to CVWs. These were joined by VA-55 (established 7 October 1983) and VA-36 (established 6 March 1987). Also under MATWING ONE was VA-42 (AD), AirLant's A-6 FRS, operating A-6E/KA-6Ds (generally totalling fifteen to twenty), as well as three TC-4Cs for training A-6 bombardier/navigators (B/Ns).

Under TACSUPWING ONE was VC-2 (JE) with nine TA-4Js, conducting target towing and adversary training until disestablishment on 30 September 1980.

Oceana's station flight (7R) had a US-2B (until 1980) and four HH-46As, the latter replaced by three SH-3Gs in 1981. A UC-12 was added in 1986.

Naval Reserve adversary squadron VC-12 (JY) was also aboard Oceana, expanding from eight to fourteen TA-4Js during 1980. It switched two TA-4Js for two A-4Fs during 1983, and another two TA-4Js for two A-4Es in 1985. VC-12 was re-designated VFC-12 (Fighter Squadron Composite) in June 1988, more accurately describing the unit's role; by then it operated seven TA-4Js and seven A-4Fs.

A VA-75 'Sunday Punchers' A-6E Intruder heading to the bombing range while on Strike Det at Fallon during 1986. It totes twelve retarded Mk 82 Snakeyes (six on each outer wing), an AGM-45 Shrike anti-radiation missile under its port wing, a LAU-10 four-tube pod for 5-in Zuni rockets under its starboard wing and a centreline external fuel tank. VA-75 was assigned to CVW-3, itself assigned to USS *John F. Kennedy*. (NARA)

A VA-35 'Black Panthers' KA-6D tanker at Fallon during a 1986 Strike Det. While the A-6 fleet was repainted in TPS, KA-6Ds were authorised to retain the old Light Gull Gray/ Insignia White scheme to aid recognition during refuelling operations. VA-35 was assigned to CVW-8/USS *Nimitz*. (NARA)

A VA-35 A-6E TRAM climbing out from Oceana during 1989, carrying Mk 76 Mod 5 25-pound practice bombs. The Target Recognition Attack Multi-Sensor (TRAM) turret, which was added to the A-6E, is evident under the nose. This contained infrared sensors and a laser designator, fully integrated with the Norden AN/APQ-148 radar (which became the AN/APQ-156 in the process). TRAM transformed the A-6E's precision attack capabilities, and resulted in laser-guided bombs (LGBs) becoming its weapon of choice. The A-6 utilised two-tone TPS: FS 36320 Dark Ghost Gray topsides, and FS 36375 Light Ghost Gray sides, undersides and the forward third of the wings. (NARA)

A VA-42 'Green Pawns' TC-4C Academe landing at Oceana during 1989. These aircraft, used to train student A-6E bombardier/navigators six at a time, featured a bulbous nose containing A-6 avionics and were also retrofitted with the TRAM sensor turret as can be seen here. (NARA)

Oceana's station flight UC-12B Huron taxies at its home station during 1989. (NARA)

Two VFC-12 'Fighting Omars' TA-4Js take off from Oceana during 1989. VFC-12 uniquely adopted overall FS 16081 Engine Gray for its A-4 fleet, only otherwise used by USN helicopters. (NARA)

Atlantic Extra-Continental Fleet Support Stations

NAS Bermuda

This was an important location for deployed ASW aircraft to monitor Soviet SSBNs on patrol. The only permanent unit was the station flight, operating a C-131F (replaced by a UP-3A during 1987) and two UH-1Ns.

Rotational deployments were made by PATWING FIVE/ELEVEN P-3C units from Brunswick/Jacksonville. VP squadrons deployed to Bermuda also often supported the US Coast Guard's Caribbean drug interdiction programme. Fleet Air Reconnaissance Squadron VQ-4 from Patuxent River maintained a regular detachment of two EC-130s at Bermuda in the TACAMO (Take Charge And Move Out) role, maintaining communications links between the National Command Authority and submerged USN SSBNs. From 1981 the full-squadron deployments by regular P-3C squadrons were augmented by half-squadron rotational deployments of Naval Reserve P-3A/B squadrons to Bermuda. From 1986 S-3 squadrons also regularly made half-squadron deployments, conducting shore-based ASW.

A P-3C of NAS Jacksonville's VP-16 'Eagles' returning to NAS Bermuda, seen in the background, while deployed there during 1985. (NARA)

NAS Guantanamo Bay, Cuba

Established under a 1903 U.S.-Cuban lease agreement, the American presence in Guantanamo Bay in southern Cuba has been disputed by the Cuban communist government since the 1959 revolution. Aboard was VC-10 (JH), which provided aerial target and adversary fleet training services with around nine TA-4Js. Due to the potential threat posed to Guantanamo Bay by Cuban forces, VC-10's TA-4Js also had an operational defensive combat role, retaining internal cannons (normally lacking from TA-4Js) and they could be armed with AIM-9 air-to-air missiles (AAMs) and

Aviation Ordnanceman 2nd Class (AO2) Robert McGill, left, AO2 John Zacko, and Aviation Ordnanceman Airman (AOAN) Lewis Ryan prepare a VC-10 'Challengers' TA-4J, armed with Mk 106 Mod 4 5-pound practice bombs, prior to a training flight from NAS Guantanamo Bay during 1983. (NARA)

Showing off VC-10's secondary defensive combat capabilities against any potential Cuban hostilities, this TPS-camouflaged TA-4J is seen during 1988 armed with five Mk 20 Rockeye II anti-armour CBUs (three on the centreline, one under each wing) and two AIM-9L/M AAMs, as well as its internal cannons. (NARA)

air-to-ground ordnance. VC-10 also operated a US-2B until 1980. Guantanamo's station flight (8F) operated three C-131Fs (reducing to two from 1981, withdrawn by 1986), two UH-1Ns and two UC-12Bs.

NAVSTA Keflavik, Iceland (later NAS Keflavik, Iceland)

Keflavik supported single P-3C squadrons, deployed rotationally. The station flight operated two C-118Bs, reducing to one in 1981 and replaced by a UP-3A in 1984.

NAF Lajes, Azores

Lajes supported half-squadron deployments by both regular P-3 units and reserve units on Active Duty for Training (ACDUTRA).

NAF Mildenhall, UK

This was a tenant at the USAF's RAF Mildenhall and supported transient USN/USMC aircraft; the station flight (8G) operated three C-131Fs, replaced by 1982 with two (from 1988 three) UC-12Bs.

NSA (Naval Support Activity) Naples, Italy

Located adjacent to Naples International Airport in Capodichino, Naples, Italy, this supported transient naval aircraft.

NAVSTA Roosevelt Roads, Puerto Rico

Aboard was VC-8 (GF), which supported training activities at the Atlantic Fleet Weapons Training Facility on Vieques Island, Puerto Rico. In 1980 it retired its three

A VMGR-252 'Heavy Haulers' KC-130F Hercules, based at MCAS Cherry Point, North Caralina, transiting through NAF Mildenhall. (Mike Freer – Touchdown Aviation, under GNU Free Documentation License 1.2)

U.S. Navy SEAL team members, and their Brazilian counterparts, rappel from a VC-8 'Redtails' SH-3G at NAVSTA Roosevelt Roads during a 1987 training exercise. (NARA)

A VC-8 TA-4J is towed by an MD-3A tow tractor on the flightline at NAVSTA Roosevelt Roads during 1986. (NARA)

drone launch and control DP-2Hs and two telemetry EP-2Hs, the last USN Neptunes in service. It retained its six TA-4Js and five (later six) SH-3Gs.

The station flight (8E) operated two US-2Bs (replaced by two UC-12Bs from 1981) and two C-131Fs, later reduced to one and retired by 1986.

NAVSTA Rota, Spain

Aboard was VQ-2 (JQ) with Electronic Intelligence (ELINT) duties, operating six EA-3Bs, six EP-3Es and one P-3A (UP-3A from 1984). EA-3B dets routinely operated from carriers on Mediterranean Sixth Fleet deployments. Following the tragic loss of a VQ-2 EA-3B and its seven crewmembers during a failed barricade landing on the USS *Nimitz* on 25 January 1987, all EA-3Bs were permanently shore-based; VQ-2 ended EA-3B sea dets in October 1987. As well as a permanent detachment in Athens, VQ-2 made periodic dets to a wide range of locations to cover the Mediterranean, the Baltic, the Indian Ocean, the Caribbean and the Persian Gulf. By 1988 VQ-2 operated nine EA-3Bs and a UA-3B, as well as the six EP-3Es and single UP-3A.

A VQ-2 'Batmen' EA-3B recovers aboard USS *Saratoga* on 22 March 1986 during operations off Libya. The VQ-2 Det had been attached to CVW-17 for *Saratoga's* August 1985 to April 1986 Mediterranean deployment. Further EA-3B VQ-2 Dets were also aboard *America* and *Coral Sea* during these operations off Libya. (NARA)

Sigonella's VR-24 (q.v.) maintained VR-24 Det Rota (JM) with four C-130Fs. In October 1984 VR-24 Det Rota became a squadron in its own right – VR-22 (JL). From 1987 VR-22 added two KC-130Fs to its four C-130Fs.

Rota also supported rotational P-3 squadron deployments.

The station flight (8D) operated a C-131F, a UC-12B and three HH-46As. From 1981 it operated a UC-12B and two SH-3Gs, soon increasing to two and three respectively. The SH-3Gs retired by 1987.

NAF Sigonella, Sicily, Italy (NAS Sigonella from 1982)

Aboard was VR-24 (JM) with transport and COD/VOD responsibilities, with three RH-53Ds, six C-1As, five C-2As and three CT-39Gs in 1980. From 1985 until decade's end VR-24 operated six C-2As and three CT-39Gs.

Established on 6 May 1983, equipped with six CH-53Es, HC-4 (HC) took over VR-24's former VOD responsibilities.

A VR-24 'Lifting Eagles' C-2A while providing carrier on-board delivery (COD) support to USS *Dwight D. Eisenhower* during 1988. (NARA)

From 1982 Sigonella supported rotationally deployed P-3 squadrons.

The facility/station flight (8C) operated two each C-1As, US-2Cs and C-131s. From 1981 it operated two C-131s and a UC-12B (four and two respectively from 1982). From 1983 it operated three C-131s (until 1986), two UC-12Bs and a VP-3A. From 1987 until decade's end it operated three UC-12s and the VP-3A.

Above left: One of VR-24's VOD RH-53Ds is seen on 26 November 1980 in Naples, Italy, preparing to deliver relief supplies to rural victims of the 23 November Irpinia earthquake. (NARA)

Above right: A HC-4 'Black Stallions' CH-53E Super Stallion lands aboard USS *Coral Sea* during VOD support operations on 21 March 1986, during operations off Libya. (NARA)

A VP-49 'Woodpeckers' P-3C flying past Mount Etna while on deployment to Sigonella during 1985. (NARA)

A VC-131G Samaritan of Sigonella's station flight. (NARA)

Pacific Continental Fleet Support Stations

Commander Naval Air Force, U.S. Pacific Fleet (COMNAVAIRPAC, 'AirPac'), at NAS North Island, provided combat-ready aviation forces to Commander-in-Chief, U.S. Pacific Fleet (CINCPACFLT). These forces were operationally controlled by the Third and Seventh Fleets (EASTPAC and WESTPAC/IO respectively).

NAS Alameda, California

MH-53E-equipped HM-15 (TB) moved to Alameda on 1 October 1987, under ASWWINGPAC (see North Island below), having been established at Norfolk on 2 January 1987.

Alameda's station flight operated three HH-46s until 1980, plus a US-2A, which was joined by a UC-12B in 1981; a second UC-12B replaced the US-2A during 1982.

Several reserve units were aboard Alameda. VR-55 (RU) had three C-9Bs. Reserve Carrier Air Wing CVWR-30 units at Alameda were VA-303, VA-304, VAK-308 and

Above: A VAK-208 'Jockeys' KA-3B performing a touch and go landing aboard USS *Dwight D. Eisenhower* during 1985. (NARA)

Left: A HM-15 'Blackhawks' MH-53E Sea Dragon tows a Mark 105 hydrofoil minesweeping sled while conducting simulated mine clearing operations in the harbour at Pohang, South Korea, during Exercise Valiant Blitz '89 in November 1989. (NARA)

Six A-4Fs of VMA-133 'Dragons' in echelon formation; just visible leading them is a VMAQ-4 'Seahawks' EA-6A from NAS Whidbey Island. The aircraft are on deployment to Fallon during 1982. Three of the A-4Fs (along with the EA-6A) are in the Light Gull Gray/Insignia White scheme, while the other three A-4Fs are in TPS. (NARA)

HS-85. VA-303 operated A-7Bs; redesignated VFA-303 on 1 January 1984, it relocated to Lemoore where it would equip with F/A-18As. A-7B-equipped VA-304 transitioned to A-7Es during 1986, then A-6Es/KA-6Ds during 1988. Tactical Aerial Refueling Squadrons VAK-208 (assigned to CVWR-20) and VAK-308 (CVWR-30) both operated around five KA-3Bs. VAK-308 disestablished on 30 September 1988; VAK-208 disestablished on 30 September 1989. HS-85 (NW) operated SH-3Ds, later SH-3Hs.

Marine reserve units were under MAG-42: VMA-133 (ME) with A-4Fs/TA-4Js (A-4Ms from 1989) and HMH-769 (MS) with CH-53As. HMH-769 disestablished 1 June 1980; its assets and CH-53As forming newly established HMH-772 Det A (MT) at Alameda (HMH-772 was headquartered at Willow Grove, Pennsylvania).

NARF Alameda (NADEP Alameda from 1987) was primarily concerned with A-3, A-6/EA-6, P-3 and S-3 major overhauls.

NAF El Centro, California

El Centro supported training deployments, including regular Training Wings One, Two and Three TA-4J detachments. The runways were marked out with simulated carrier deck landing areas, complete with fresnel lens optical landing system (FLOLS) 'meatballs' for carrier qualification (CARQUAL) training. Many USN and USMC active/reserve squadrons deployed to use the nearby bombing ranges or to conduct air-to-air gunnery training against targets towed behind A-4s. The Navy Flight Demonstration Squadron (NFDS) 'Blue Angels' used El Centro as their winter training home, with their A-4F/TA-4Js (F/A-18A/Bs from 1987) and supporting KC-130F. The base flight (8N) operated a contract rented Cessna 402C from 1982, replaced by a rented Piper Navajo PA-31 during 1986, itself replaced by a UC-12B in 1988.

NAS Fallon, Nevada

Fallon also primarily supported training deployments. VA-122, the Lemoore-based AirPac A-7 FRS, maintained 'VA-122 Detachment Fallon' (NJ) at the station until

Seen preparing for a sortie on the Fallon ramp during 1988 is an F/A-18C of VFA-106 Detachment Fallon. In the foreground is an F/A-18D from an unidentified unit, while in the background is an F-5E of VFA-127 'Cylons' and an O-2A of VFA-125 Detachment Fallon. (NARA)

1985. Lemoore's VFA-125, the AirPac F/A-18 FRS, established 'VFA-125 Detachment Fallon' (NJ) in 1984. VA-122 Detachment Fallon received six range control O-2As during 1983; in 1986 they transferred to VFA-125 Detachment Fallon. Cecil Field's VFA-106, AirLant's F/A-18 FRS, established VFA-106 'Detachment Fallon' (AD) in 1985. Adversary squadron VFA-127 (NJ) moved to Fallon from Lemoore on 1 October 1987, with a mixed A-4F/TA-4J, F-5E/F and T-38A/QT-38A fleet.

The Naval Strike Warfare Center (NSWC), known as Strike University or 'Strike-U', was established at Fallon in October 1984, to evaluate and refine existing strike tactics, develop new ones, and train squadron and air wing strike leaders to get the most from their weapons systems. It was established following the disastrous December 1983 Beirut strikes (q.v.). Strike-U ran an intensive ten-day Strike Leader Attack Training Syllabus (SLATS) academic course, each for up to fifty-four officers. Its other major activity was supporting 'Strike Det': detachments to Fallon by full CVWs (LANTFLT and PACFLT). The eighteen-day Strike Det focussed on integration of the CVW, therefore all of the CVW's squadrons were deployed. This included the S-3 and SH-3 squadrons; while they could not practice their ASW role in Nevada they conducted conventional bombing and SAR training respectively. AirLant SH-3 squadrons didn't make the long journey across country with their helicopters, instead borrowing HH-3As from North Island's HC-9.

A Naval Strike Warfare Center (NSWC), or 'Strike-U', A-7E seen during 1987. (NARA)

A NSWC F/A-18A seen taking off during 1989; note the AN/AAS-38 FLIR pod on the port fuselage pylon, which would otherwise carry the AIM-7 Sparrow. Barely visible on the starboard fuselage pylon is an ASQ-173 Laser Detector Tracker/Camera (LDT/CAM) pod; this spots targets that have been illuminated by laser designators and was related to the USAF's Pave Penny pod used on A-10As and A-7Ds. (NARA)

A Fallon station flight SAR HH-1N during a 1983 search and rescue exercise. (NARA)

Strike-U had a number of aircraft directly assigned, initially two each A-6Es, A-7Es and F/A-18As; by 1989, two A-6Es, three A-7Es, two TA-7Cs and five F/A-18As.

Fallon's station flight (7H) operated a US-2A and a US-2B (both retired during 1981) along with two (later up to four) HH-1Ns. A UC-12B was added in 1988, operating this alongside two HH-1Ns by 1989.

NAS Lemoore, California

Light Attack Wing Pacific (LATWINGPAC) aboard Lemoore, administratively controlled AirPac's deployable A-7E squadrons, which were operationally assigned to CVWs: VA-22, VA-25, VA-27, VA-94, VA-97, VA-113, VA-146, VA-147, VA-192 and VA-195, each with around twelve A-7Es.

Also under LATWINGPAC was VA-122 (NJ), AirPac's A-7 FRS, and training/adversary squadron VA-127 (NJ), joined in 1980 by VFA-125 (NJ), the F/A-18 FRS.

VA-122 peaked during 1981 with twenty-seven TA-7Cs and twenty-four A-7Es (numbers declining late in the decade as A-7 training wound down), along with a T-39D (retained until 1984). As noted previously, VA-122 Detachment Fallon

A VA-27 'Royal Maces' A-7E assigned to CVW-14, and armed with six live Mk 82 Snakeyes, prepares to launch from USS *Coral Sea* on New Year's Day 1980, during hostage crisis operations off Iran. *Coral Sea* was conducting a November 1979 to June 1980 WESTPAC/Indian Ocean deployment. Green shirt catapult crew, a red shirt Aviation Ordnanceman, and a white shirt/green cranial (helmet) squadron plane inspector undertake their respective duties. (NARA)

A VA-94 'Mighty Shrikes' A-7E, and CVW-15's CAG bird, visiting NAS Cubi Point on 1 May 1981. CVW-15 was assigned to USS *Kitty Hawk* (CV-63), which was on an April to November 1981 WESTPAC deployment at the time. Following this deployment CVW-15 was reorganised, with VA-94 reassigned to CVW-11 aboard USS *Enterprise* (CVN-65). (NARA)

VA-94's sister A-7 squadron within CVW-15 aboard USS *Kitty Hawk* was VA-22 'Fighting Redcocks'. This VA-22 A-7E conducts a tanker mission, equipped with the D-704 'buddy pod' aerial refuelling store, during the same 1981 WESTPAC cruise as the VA-94 A-7E in the previous image. When CVW-15 was subsequently reorganised, VA-22 remained paired with VA-94, and joined CVW-11 aboard USS *Enterprise*. (NARA)

The VA-94 A-7E, BuNo 159989/'NH-401', of squadron CO Cdr Carl W 'Tad' Chamberlain, at Fallon for Strike Det with CVW-11 during 1987. By now, even the CO's bird was in subdued TPS camouflage. The following year, during Operation *Praying Mantis*, Cdr Chamberlain led the joint VA-22/94 six-aircraft 'War at Sea' package against the Iranian frigate *Sahand* in this A-7E. (NARA)

The VA-22 CO's A-7E also at Fallon during the same 1987 Strike Det as seen in the previous image. This aircraft, BuNo 160537/'NH-301', had received this one-off experimental camouflage scheme earlier that year. This aircraft was transferred out of VA-22 later in 1987. The CO's replacement A-7E, BuNo 158833/'NH-301', participated in Operation *Praying Mantis* and, towards the end of CVW-11's 1988 deployment aboard USS *Enterprise*, subsequently received an almost identical experimental camouflage scheme to that seen here. (NARA)

received six range control O-2As during 1983, transferred to VFA-125 Detachment Fallon in 1986.

VA-127 was responsible for basic refresher all weather jet instrument training, air combat manoeuvring adversary training, foreign pilot training, and jet transition/ refresher training; from 1983 adversary training became its primary role. During 1980 it added an A-4F to its existing TA-4F/J fleet, but retained a primarily two-seat fleet while at Lemoore. VA-127 was redesignated VFA-127 on 1 March 1987 and moved to Fallon on 1 October 1987, where it added F-5s/T-38s to its fleet.

VFA-125, the first F/A-18 squadron, established on 13 November 1980 at Lemoore under LATWINGPAC. It initially served as a joint USN/USMC training unit, also training foreign F/A-18 pilots and conducting operational trials; after the activation of VFA-106 (AirLant F/A-18 FRS at Cecil Field) and VMFAT-101 at El Toro (USMC F/A-18 training unit), VFA-125 became AirPac's F/A-18 FRS. VFA-125 initially received small numbers of F/A-18As and TF-18As (later redesignated F/A-18Bs) and also operated a handful of A-7Es until 1982. By 1984 VFA-125 operated twenty-two F/A-18A/Bs, peaking at fifty-four during 1985, with forty-seven in service in 1989.

Yellow shirt plane directors position a VFA-125 'Rough Riders' F/A-18B on the flight deck of USS *Carl Vinson* (CVN-70), while another approaches to trap aboard, during student Hornet pilot training in 1984. (NARA)

While F/A-18As replaced A-7Es during the 1980s, USMC and AirLant USN squadrons were prioritised ahead of LATWINGPAC squadrons. Therefore VA-22, VA-27, VA-94 and VA-97 retained A-7Es for the remainder of the 1980s. VA-113 and VA-25 became VFA-113/VFA-25 on 25 March and 1 July 1983 respectively, re-equipped with F/A-18As. VF-161, hitherto an F-4S-equipped squadron assigned to CVW-5 at Atsugi, Japan, joined LATWINGPAC at Lemoore on 17 June 1986, redesignated as VFA-161 with F/A-18As. Operationally assigned to the short-lived CVW-10, cutbacks saw it disestablished on 1 April 1988. VA-147/VA-146 were redesignated VFA-147/VFA-146 on 20/21 July 1989 respectively and re-equipped with F/A-18As.

Several other squadrons joined LATWINGPAC for F/A-18 training before being reassigned elsewhere. VFA-131 and VFA-132 were established under LATWINGPAC on 3 October 1983 and 9 January 1984 respectively; once trained by VFA-125, they were reassigned in February 1985 to LATWING ONE/AirLant at Cecil Field. VA-195 and VA-192 were redesignated VFA-195/VFA-192 on 1 April 1985 and 10 January 1986 respectively, moving to Atsugi during November 1986 to serve with CVW-5. VF-151, previously an F-4S-equipped CVW-5/Atsugi squadron, was redesignated VFA-151 at Lemoore with LATWINGPAC on 17 June 1986; it returned to Atsugi, along with VFA-192/VFA-195, during November 1986.

A VFA-113 'Stingers' F/A-18A, complete with AIS pod on the wingtip Sidewinder pylon, at Fallon for Strike Det during 1986. VFA-113 was assigned to CVW-14 aboard USS *Constellation* (CV-64). (NARA)

A VFA-303 'Golden Hawks' F/A-18A over Southern California during 1989. Reserve squadron VFA-303 was assigned to CVWR-30. (NARA)

Former A-7B-equipped reserve squadron VA-303 moved from Alameda to Lemoore on 1 January 1984. Redesignated VFA-303, it finally received its initial eight F/A-18As on 19 October 1985, building up to twelve by 1988.

Lemoore's station flight (7S) operated a C-1A, two US-2Bs and four (from 1983 just two) UH-1Ns. During 1982 the C-1A and US-2Bs were replaced by two UC-12Bs.

NAS Miramar, California

Fighter/Airborne Early Warning Wing Pacific (FITAEWWINGPAC) aboard Miramar, administratively controlled deployable squadrons, which were operationally assigned to CVWs. These were Fighter Squadrons VF-1, VF-2, VF-21, VF-24, VF-51, VF-111, VF-114, VF-154, VF-211 and VF-213, Light Photographic Squadron VFP-63 and AEW Squadrons VAW-112, VAW-113, VAW-114, VAW-116 and VAW-117. VF-21 and VF-154 were F-4S-equipped at the start of the decade, transitioning to F-4Ns in 1981 ahead of a final F-4 cruise on USS *Coral Sea*. They subsequently transitioned to F-14As, completing

A VF-51 'Screaming Eagles' F-14A intercepts a Soviet Naval Aviation Tu-95RTs 'Bear-D' maritime reconnaissance/targeting aircraft, which was investigating the *Kitty Hawk* carrier battle group on 15 October 1979. VF-51 was assigned to CVW-15, and this was during that air wing's May 1979 to February 1980 WESTPAC deployment aboard USS *Kitty Hawk*. A live AIM-54 is visible under the F-14A, while an AIM-7 can just be seen under the port wing; it lacks external fuel tanks. (NARA)

A VF-142 'Ghostriders' F-14A thumps onto the deck of USS *Dwight D. Eisenhower* during CVW-7's October 1984 to May 1985 Mediterranean deployment. It has caught the number two arrestor wire, or 'cross deck pendant' (the second from the stern, of four); this is acceptable, but the three-wire was the preferred one to catch. To catch the one-wire, nearest the stern round-down, was frowned upon, usually receiving a poor landing grade from the Landing Signals Officer (LSO); catching the four-wire was also undesirable as it indicated that the landing was high, but at least safer than catching a one-wire. (NARA)

Four VF-2 'Bounty Hunters' F-14As, including the colourful CO's bird, in formation while returning from USS *Ranger* (CV-61) to Miramar during December 1987. VF-2 was assigned to CVW-2, and had just completed a July to December 1987 WESTPAC/IO deployment aboard *Ranger*. (NARA)

A VF-1 'Wolfpack' F-14A, CVW-2's CAG bird, seen preparing to launch on a training sortie at Fallon during a September 1988 Strike Det. It is equipped with an inert captive training Sidewinder and an AIS pod. (NARA)

A VF-211 'Fighting Checkmates' F-14A+ displays a full load of six CATM-54Cs (captive training AIM-54Cs) during an October 1989 flight from Miramar. This loadout would be too heavy to recover with aboard a carrier, without dumping several of the expensive missiles if unused. Therefore this land-based demonstration load was impractical for actual carrier-borne use. VF-211 had just transitioned from F-14A to F-14A+, and was assigned to CVW-9 aboard USS *Nimitz*. The General Electric F110-GE-400-powered F-14A+ (redesignated F-14B in 1991) was an interim improved Tomcat, pending the definitive F-14D, which would not enter service until late 1990. (NARA)

conversion during 1984. The other Fighter Squadrons were already F-14-equipped at the start of the decade. Two additional, short-lived F-14A squadrons, VF-191 and VF-194 were established on 1 December 1986 (not actually receiving their first F-14As until 6 April 1987) to serve with equally short-lived CVW-10; they disestablished on 30 April 1988. VF-24 and VF-211 transitioned from F-14As to improved F-14A+s during 1989.

RF-8G-equipped VFP-63 sent small dets to sea with both LANTFLT and PACFLT CVWs until it disestablished on 30 June 1982. When F-14As took over the reconnaissance mission from RF-8Gs, VF-2, VF-111, VF-154, VF-211 and VF-213 were the AirPac squadrons to receive TARPS-wired F-14As, usually three being so-equipped per squadron.

VAW-114 and VAW-116 already operated E-2Cs by 1980. VAW-112, VAW-113 and VAW-117 were still E-2B-equipped, transitioning to E-2Cs during 1980, 1984 and 1981 respectively. VAW-111 established on 1 October 1986 with E-2Cs to serve with CVW-10, but disestablished on 30 April 1988.

A VAW-112 'Golden Hawks' E-2C at Fallon during an April 1988 Strike Det; VAW-112 was assigned to CVW-9 aboard USS *Nimitz*. (NARA)

Several permanent squadrons were also under FITAEWWINGPAC:

RVAW-110 (TT squadron identification letters replaced by NJ during 1980), redesignated VAW-110 on 1 May 1983, was AirPac's E-2 FRS. For most of the decade it operated between nine and twelve E-2s, with seven E-2Bs and two TE-2As in early 1980; that year it received its first two E-2Cs, replacing two E-2Bs. E-2Cs completely replaced the remaining E-2Bs and TE-2As by late 1985. From 1988 VAW-110 also took on C-2A training, with three assigned.

VF-121 (NJ), AirPac's F-4 FRS, with eleven F-4Js, disestablished on 30 September 1980.

VF-124 (NJ), AirPac's F-14 FRS, operated around forty F-14As in 1980, with around thirty for the remainder of the decade.

During the first half of the decade, adversary squadron VF-126 (NJ) operated around thirteen (later eleven) TA-4Js and three A-4Fs, plus three spin training T-2Cs. In 1985 VF-126 added three F-5Es and a T-38A. During 1987/88 it reduced its TA-4J fleet, added A-4Es/TA-4Fs and replaced its F-5Es/T-38A with F-16Ns. In 1989 it operated six/four A-4E/Fs, four/four TA-4F/Js, six F-16Ns and four T-2Cs.

VC-7 (UH) operated four A-4Fs and six/two TA-4F/Js for training support duties, including target towing, until being disestablished on 30 September 1980.

The US Navy Fighter Weapons School (NFWS), known as TOPGUN, trained USN and USMC fighter air crews at graduate level in all aspects of fighter weapons systems, including tactics, techniques, procedures and doctrine. Graduates returned to their squadrons, spreading their knowledge throughout the fleet. Students attending TOPGUN used aircraft from their own squadron to participate; TOPGUN instructors operated a fleet of adversary aircraft to support this training. In 1980 TOPGUN operated six A-4Es, an A-4F, six F-5Es and three F-5Fs; by 1985 it operated four A-4Es, one NA-4F, five F-5Es and three F-5Fs. Six F-16Ns and two TF-16Ns replaced TOPGUN's F-5E/Fs during 1988, joining the then remaining five A-4Es and single NA-4F. Five additional A-4Fs were added to TOPGUN's fleet during mid- to late 1989.

The success of TOPGUN inspired the creation of a similar E-2 community weapons school, the Carrier Airborne Early Warning Weapons School (CAEWWS), or TOPDOME, which was established on 13 July 1988, also under FITAEWWINGPAC at Miramar.

TOPGUN A-4E, BuNo 150023 ('56'), featuring 'MARINES' titles during 1984. In 1983 this A-4E had been repainted in this 'Heater-Ferris' deceptive camouflage scheme (named for its creators, TOPGUN's Lt Cmdr Chuck 'Heater' Heatley and aviation artist Keith Ferris), consisting of diagonal stripes of colour. The USN was experimenting with variations of this scheme at this time. It consisted of FS 36495 Light Gray, FS 36307 Light Sea Gray, FS 35237 Gray Blue and FS 35164 Intermediate Blue. A second TOPGUN A-4E would receive this scheme during 1984. (NARA)

A TOPGUN F-5E Tiger II. As TOPGUN included both USN and USMC Instructors, and trained students from both services, several of its assigned aircraft carried 'MARINES' titles. Many widely varying camouflage schemes were adopted by TOPGUN adversary aircraft, and these were periodically changed. A CATM-9L (Captive Air Training Missile) – an inert, captive training version of the live AIM-9L Sidewinder – is on the F-5E's wingtip. A VF-101 'Grim Reapers' F-14A is seen in formation in this 1984 scene. (NARA)

Right: Another TOPGUN F-5E seen during 1984, in yet another scheme, but this time with more usual 'NAVY' titles. Again this F-5E features a wingtip CATM-9L. (NARA)

Below: A TOPGUN F-16N awaits its turn to launch while F-14As approach the Miramar runway during 1989. Almost completely blocked from view behind the F-16N are an F/A-18 and a TOPGUN A-4. (NARA)

The station flight operated a C-1A until 1982.

Naval Air Reserve squadrons at Miramar were CVWR-30's VF-301, VF-302 and VAW-88, plus VC-13.

VF-301 transitioned from F-4N to F-4S during spring 1981, then to the F-14A during 1985.

VF-302 transitioned from F-4N to F-4S during November 1980, then to the F-14A in March 1985; three of VF-302's twelve F-14As were wired for TARPS.

VAW-88 transitioned from E-2B to E-2C during 1987.

VC-13 (UX) operated as an adversary squadron with TA-4Js, operating around fourteen until 1984; that year A-4Es joined VC-13 and around ten TA-4Js and four A-4Es were operated until 1987 when seven of each were in use. On 22 April 1988 the squadron was redesignated VFC-13; during that year A-4Fs replaced the A-4Es.

A pair of F-4S Phantom IIs from VF-301 Devil's Disciples during 1984. Both of Miramar's Naval Air Reserve fighter squadrons, VF-301 and VF-302, applied variations of trial 'Heater-Ferris' camouflage to several of their F-4S aircraft from 1983. It consisted of FS 36375 Light Ghost Gray, FS 36307 Light Sea Gray, FS 35237 Blue Gray and FS 35164 Intermediate Blue. VF-301 used black markings as seen here, while VF-302 used grey markings on its 'Heater-Ferris' camouflaged jets. (NARA)

A TPS camouflaged TA-4J of VFC-13, seen on the Miramar flight line during 1988. (NARA)

NAS Moffett Field, California

Aboard Moffett Field were the deployable Patrol Squadrons under Patrol Wings Pacific (PATWINGSPAC), until PATWING TEN was established to control them on 1 June 1981 (PATWING TEN subsequently serving as the link between patrol squadrons and PATWINGSPAC): VP-9 (PD), VP-19 (PE), VP-40 (QE), VP-46 (RC), VP-47 (RD), VP-48 (SF) and VP-50 (SG), each with nine P-3Cs. Additionally VP-31 (RP), AirPac's P-3 FRS, was assigned directly to PATWINGSPAC throughout. In early 1980 VP-31 operated one P-3A, seven P-3Bs, three P-3B TACNAVMODs (P-3Bs updated with some P-3C systems through the Tactical-Navigation Modernization programme) and twelve P-3Cs. On 25 July 1984 VP-31 received the USN's first, much improved, P-3C Update III; it soon commenced training VP-40 in the new variant in preparation for the latter becoming the first fleet operational squadron to receive Update IIIs. In 1985 VP-31 operated one VP-3A, three P-3B TACNAVMODs and seventeen P-3Cs (a mixture of baseline and Update sub-variants). By 1989 VP-31 operated one UP-3A, five TP-3As, three P-3B TACNAVMODs, five baseline P-3Cs, two P-3C Update Is and four P-3C Update IIIs.

Naval Air Reserve squadron VP-91 (PM) was also aboard Moffett Field with P-3Bs, transitioning to P-3B TACNAVMODs from 1985.

VP-MAU Moffett (PS) was established on 20 December 1986, like the original VP-MAU at Brunswick, its reserve crews would augment regular Moffett VP squadrons if mobilised. By 1989 VP-MAU Moffett operated two TP-3As and a P-3C.

A VP-50 'Blue Dragons' P-3C taxis to Moffett Field's runway during the squadron's annual mine readiness certification inspection in 1985. Under the outer wing are a Mk 56 air-delivered moored mine (inboard) and a Mk 62 Quickstrike mine (outboard), the latter related to the Mk 82 general purpose bomb. (NARA)

Two VP-31 'Black Lightnings' P-3Cs in flight during 1987. (NARA)

NAS North Island, California

Aboard North Island was Anti-Submarine Warfare Wing Pacific (ASWWINGPAC), primarily controlling deployable HS, HSL, HC and VS Squadrons.

HS-2 transitioned from SH-3Ds to SH-3Hs during 1980; HS-4, HS-6, HS-8 and HS-12 were already operating SH-3Hs by 1980. Each squadron generally had six airframes. HS-12 was reassigned to CVW-5 at Atsugi in July 1984. Two additional SH-3H squadrons joined them during the decade: HS-14, established 10 July 1984 and HS-16 established 10 March 1987. HS-16 was assigned to short-lived CVW-10, and soon disestablished 1 June 1988.

An HS-6 'Indians' SH-3H, trailing its AN/ASQ-81(V)-2 Magnetic Anomaly Detector (MAD) 'bird' from the starboard sponson, on 13 July 1983. It retains the Light Gull Gray/Insignia White scheme, but with toned-down markings pending the switch to TPS. HS-6 was assigned to CVW-11 aboard USS *Enterprise*. (NARA)

An HS-2 'Golden Falcons' SH-3H seen on 30 January 1987. HS-2 was assigned to CVW-9 aboard USS *Kitty Hawk* (just visible on the horizon), which was conducting a January to June 1987 'world cruise' from San Diego to Norfolk, ahead of *Kitty Hawk's* temporary assignment to LANTFLT while she underwent SLEP at Philadelphia. (NARA)

An HS-14 'Chargers' SH-3H, in TPS camouflage, on Strike Det at Fallon on 23 September 1988, with CVW-2, which was assigned to USS *Ranger*. SH-3 squadrons practiced their SAR duties while participating in Strike Det, being unable to practice their ASW role in land-locked Nevada. (NARA)

HSL-33 (TF) and HSL-35 (TG) operated SH-2Fs; these were joined by HSL-43 (TT, established 5 October 1984), HSL-45 (TZ, established 3 October 1986) and HSL-47 (TY, established 25 September 1987) with SH-60Bs.

HC-1 (UP) primarily operated SH-3Gs, briefly adding small numbers of SH-3Ds during 1981/82 and 1989, an SH-3A during 1983 and SH-3Hs in 1989; CH-53Es joined from 10 January 1984. In 1989 HC-1 operated two SH-3Ds, twelve SH-3Gs, one SH-3H and four CH-53Es. HC-1 also maintained permanent Dets at Atsugi and Diego Garcia (q.v.). HC-3 (SA) operated HH-46As (until 1987) alongside CH-46Ds, adding CH-46As during 1985–86, and HH-46Ds from 1987. In 1989 it operated seven CH-46D and six HH-46D. As well as providing utility/transport and SAR services, it was also AirPac's H-46 FRS. HC-11 (VR) operated CH-46Ds, adding HH-46As from 1982. By 1989 it operated six CH-46Ds, twelve HH-46Ds and four UH-46Ds.

S-3A-equipped squadrons were VS-21, VS-29, VS-33, VS-37 and VS-38. These were joined by VS-35, which was established 10 March 1987 but disestablished on 1 June 1988, again assigned to CVW-10 during its brief existence.

Various permanent ASWWINGPAC squadrons were also aboard North Island:

VS-41 (NJ), AirPac's S-3 FRS, operated around thirty S-3As, reducing to around twenty in the latter part of the decade. The sole KS-3A was also assigned until 1985 (subsequently reconfigured as a US-3A and reassigned to VRC-50 with which it was lost in a fatal crash on 20 January 1989).

VC-3 (UF) operated three DC-130As and provided target drone services until disestablishment on 1 October 1981.

VRC-30 (RW) primarily operated up to ten COD C-1As, alongside two or three CT-39E/Gs. A UC-12B joined during 1982. During 1986 C-2As replaced the C-1As. By 1989 VRC-30 operated a UC-12B, a UC-12F, three CT-39Es and seven C-2A(R)s.

Also seen during CVW-2's Strike Det at Fallon on 23 September 1988 is this VS-38 'Red Griffins' S-3A. (NARA)

A VRC-30 'Providers' C-2A preparing for take-off from North Island on 23 December 1986. (NARA)

HSL-31 (TD), AirPac's H-2 FRS, operated ten or eleven H-2s, predominantly SH-2Fs, periodically operating single SH-2Ds/HH-2Ds.

HS-10 (RA), AirPac's H-3 FRS, operated six each SH-3Ds and SH-3Hs in 1980. From 1981 onwards SH-3Hs dominated, with small numbers of SH-3As, SH-3Ds and HH-3As periodically assigned. In June 1989 HS-10's last SH-3H students completed training; on 1 October 1989, HS-10 became the first SH-60F FRS. The SH-60F was being introduced to replace SH-3Hs in HS Squadrons. Five SH-60Fs were assigned to HS-10 in 1989, the first arriving on 22 June.

HSL-41 (TS) established 21 January 1983 as AirPac's SH-60B FRS. It built up to full strength of around fifteen aircraft by 1985.

A newly received SH-60F of HS-10 'Taskmasters' lowers its AN/AQS-13F dipping sonar into the Pacific Ocean during late 1989. The AN/AQS-13F was an updated version of the AN/AQS-13E used by the SH-3H that the SH-60F was replacing. (NARA)

An HSL-41 'Sea Hawks' SH-60B approaching the landing pad of the Oliver Hazard Perry-class guided missile frigate USS *Crommelin* (FFG-37) on 12 October 1983. The SH-60B's AN/ASQ-81 MAD bird is visible on the starboard rear fuselage. (NARA)

Finally under ASWWINGPAC control was the station flight (7M) operating two U-11As. During 1980 a UC-12B was added and a second UC-12B replaced one of the U-11As during 1981. From 1982 only the two UC-12Bs remained.

NARF North Island (NADEP North Island from 1987) was primarily concerned with F-4 and F/A-18 major overhauls.

A North Island station
flight U-11A Aztec.
(NARA)

Reserve units aboard North Island were as follows:

NARU North Island operated two C-131Fs, dropping to one during 1980, which
was retired mid-decade. VR-57 (RX) operated three C-9Bs. HC-9 operated up to
nine HH-3As in the combat search and rescue (CSAR) role. HS-84 (NW) operated
up to eight SH-3Ds; HS-84 became HSL-84 in April 1984, equipped with seven
SH-2Fs.

A HC-9 'Protectors'
HH-3A seen over the
Californian coast during
1983. (NARA)

NAS Whidbey Island, Washington

Aboard Whidbey Island were the VA (medium) and VAQ squadrons of Medium Attack/Tactical Electronic Warfare Wing Pacific (MATVAQWINGPAC).

Deployable Attack Squadrons were VA-52, VA-95, VA-145, VA-165 and VA-196, generally equipped with up to ten A-6Es and four KA-6Ds; VA-155 was established on 1 September 1987 with A-6Es only. Additionally, VA-185 was established on 1 December 1986, but once trained it left for Atsugi during September 1987 to join CVW-5.

A VA-165 'Boomers' KA-6D refuels a VAQ-134 'Garudas' EA-6B in February 1982. Both squadrons were assigned to CVW-9 aboard USS *Constellation*, which was conducting an October 1981 to May 1982 WESTPAC/IO deployment. (NARA)

A VA-145 'Swordsmen' A-6E at Fallon for Strike Det during September 1988. While most VA-145 A-6s carried sword fin markings, several, including this example, carried a rampant beast, which was also featured in the squadron's insignia. This A-6E carries a load of live Mk 82 Snakeyes, and just visible behind them is an AIS pod for use over the range. VA-145 was assigned to CVW-2, which was in turn assigned to USS *Ranger*. (NARA)

MATVAQWINGPAC held all deployable VAQ squadrons, for operational employment by both LANTFLT and PACFLT CVWs: VAQ-130, VAQ-131, VAQ-132, VAQ-133, VAQ-134, VAQ-135, VAQ-136 (moving to Atsugi with CVW-5 in February 1980), VAQ-137 and VAQ-138, each generally with four EA-6Bs. These were joined by VAQ-139 (established 1 July 1983), VAQ-140 (established 1 October 1985), VAQ-141 (established 1 July 1987) and VAQ-142 (established 1 June 1988).

A VAQ-130 'Zappers' EA-6B Prowler over the Pacific on 1 December 1985. At this time VAQ-130 was assigned to CVW-2, which had by now been reassigned to USS *Kitty Hawk*. *Kitty Hawk* was conducting a July to December 1985 WESTPAC/ IO deployment. (NARA)

An AIS pod-equipped EA-6B of VAQ-138 'Yellowjackets' at Fallon for Strike Det on 1 April 1986. VAQ-138 was assigned to LANTFLT's CVW-8 aboard USS *Nimitz* at this time. The blotchy appearance of this aircraft is typical of TPS aircraft that have had their paint touched up during corrosion work. (NARA)

Permanent MATVAQWINGPAC units were VA-128, VAQ-129 and the station flight. VA-128 (NJ) was AirPac's A-6 FRS, fluctuating between fifteen A-6Es at the start of the decade and thirty by decade's end. It also periodically had a KA-6D assigned and two, later four, TC-4Cs. VAQ-129 (NJ) was the EA-6B FRS with around eight EA-6Bs, rising to around sixteen by decade's end. The station flight (7G) initially operated a C-1A, a US-2B and three, soon four, HH-46As. During 1981 it re-equipped with two UC-12Bs and three SH-3Ds; a third UC-12B was added in 1988.

The following Naval Reserve squadrons were aboard Whidbey Island: VP-69 (PJ) operated P-3As, peaking at eleven aircraft during 1985; a detachment of NAS Glenview-based VR-51 (RV) operated four C-118Bs from Whidbey until the det disestablished in 1982. VR-61 (RS), established on 16 October 1982, operated two leased ex-airline DC-9-31s (in lieu of purpose-built C-9Bs); VAQ-309 operated five EA-6As until replacing them with EA-6Bs from 2 December 1989.

Whidbey Island's Marine Reserve unit was initially HML-770 (MN) with eleven UH-1Ns, under 'Det MAG-46, Whidbey Island'. The unit disestablished in 1980, but its assets remained briefly and formed HML-767 Det A (MM), still under Det MAG-46, Whidbey Island until 1981 (HML-767 was headquartered aboard NAS New Orleans). Marine Tactical Electronic Warfare Squadron VMAQ-4 (RM) was established under MAG-42 Det C on 21 May 1981, with four or five EA-6As.

A Marine Reserve UH-1N of HML-770 on the flight line while visiting Naval Education and Training Command Station NAS Whiting Field. (NARA)

Pacific Extra-Continental Fleet Support Stations

NAVSTA Adak, Alaska

NAVSTA Adak (from 1984 NAS Adak), in the North Pacific's Aleutian Islands, accommodated rotational PATWINGSPAC P-3 squadron three or four aircraft detachments; from 1985 full squadron (nine aircraft) rotational deployments were made.

In 1989 a station flight operating a single C-130 was established.

NAS Agana, Guam

VQ-1 (PR, although EA-3B sea dets often adopted the CVW's identification letters, and from 1988 squadron markings and identification letters were removed), under Fleet Air West Pacific (FAIRWESTPAC), conducted fleet-support electronic reconnaissance throughout the Pacific, from the U.S. West Coast to the African East Coast. It operated both land and sea detachments. Routine land detachments were made (primarily by EP-3B/Es, sometimes by EA-3Bs) to Atsugi, Cubi Point, Diego Garcia, Kadena and Misawa, and sometimes further afield to locations such as Ambouli, Djibouti and Muscat, Oman. Meanwhile, EA-3B sea dets were made to carriers, until EA-3B sea dets were curtailed in November 1987; in November 1988 VQ-1 relinquished its EA-3Bs.

Like its AirLant sister-squadron VQ-2, VQ-1's specific duties included Electronic Support Measures (ESM) protection and early warning for Carrier Battle Groups (CVBGs), radio frequency (RF) 'leakage checks' for surface units (ensuring RF

This VQ-1 'World Watchers' EA-3B is seen while attached to CVW-15 (forming 'VQ-1 Det.C' and having adopted CVW-15's 'NL' identification letters) aboard USS *Carl Vinson* during her October 1984 to May 1985 WESTPAC/ IO deployment. The EA-3B is being prepared to launch from *Carl Vinson's* No. 4 waist catapult. (NARA)

discipline), and early detection of non-U.S. reconnaissance aircraft (e.g. picking up transmissions from Soviet Tu-95RTs 'Bear-D' reconnaissance aircraft). They supported both sides during exercises (including, for example, EP-3s simulating a Tu-16 'Badger', with EA-3Bs simulating the Badger's anti-ship AS-5 missiles), while conducting EW protection of the exercise itself. PARPRO (Peacetime Airborne Reconnaissance Program) missions supporting fleet and national tasking were flown in the Northern Pacific, Sea of Japan, Sea of Okhotsk and Korea; some missions were co-ordinated with USAF reconnaissance aircraft.

In 1980 VQ-1 operated eight EA-3Bs, one TA-3B, two EP-3Bs, four EP-3Es and a P-3B; the TA-3B and P-3B were utilised for training and VIP transport. During 1982 the TA-3B was replaced by a VA-3B and the P-3B by two P-3As. On 23 January 1985 VQ-1's Commanding Officer, CDR John T. Mitchell, was flying the unit's VA-3B (BuNo 142672/'PR-111') from Guam to Atsugi, with eight other unit personnel aboard. The aircraft reported problems with its air turbine motors, which powered the hydraulic pumps, in turn powering the flight controls. Soon thereafter, and 125 nautical miles north of Guam, the VA-3B disappeared from radar screens. No trace of the aircraft or its occupants was ever found. In 1985, following the VA-3B's loss, VQ-1 operated seven EA-3Bs, two EP-3Bs, four EP-3Es, a P-3A and two UP-3As. The EP-3Bs were withdrawn by 1988, leaving six EA-3Bs, four EP-3Es and three UP-3As; the EA-3Bs were withdrawn that November.

Also under FAIRWESTPAC was VQ-3 (TC) with two TACAMO EC-130Qs and a KC-130F aboard Agana, until the squadron moved to Barbers Point during 1980.

Det 105 of North Island's HC-3 relocated with its two CH-46s from Atsugi to Agana during 1981, remaining there until its utility/transport/SAR responsibilities were taken on by HC-5 (RB), newly established aboard Agana on 3 February 1984 under FAIRWESTPAC. HC-5 operated ten CH-46As, from 1985 twelve HH-46As.

Finally under FAIRWESTPAC, the station flight operated a C-117D, replaced by a UC-12B during 1980, and two (from 1981 three) UH-1Ns, although the latter were withdrawn by 1985.

PATWING ONE, located at Naval Support Facility (NAVSUPPFA) Kamiseya, Japan, had no squadrons assigned, but exercised operational control of VP squadrons deployed to the region; it maintained PATWING ONE DET AGANA, supporting rotational P-3 dets to Agana.

A HC-5 'Providers' HH-46A conducting VERTREP operations during 1987. This HH-46A is being guided in by a crewman to retrieve supplies from her assigned ship, the Mars-class combat stores ship USS *Niagara Falls* (AFS-3). (NARA)

NAF Atsugi, Japan

CVW-5, the only CVW forward-deployed outside the U.S.A., and under FAIRWESTPAC control, was shore-based aboard Atsugi; CVW-5 was assigned to USS *Midway* homeported at nearby Yokosuka. CVW-5 was assigned F-4J-equipped VF-151 and VF-161 (re-equipped with F-4S between December 1980 and February 1981), A-7E-equipped VA-56 and VA-93, A-6E/KA-6D-equipped VA-115, E-2B-equipped VAW-115 (E-2Cs from 1985) and an SH-3G-equipped HC-1 detachment (HC-1 Det 2). SH-3H-equipped HS-12 moved from North Island to Atsugi in July 1984, replacing HC-1 Det 2 within CVW-5. The USMC initially provided Reconnaissance/ECM detachments; a Marine Tactical Reconnaissance Squadron VMFP-3 RF-4B det (until 1984) and a VMAQ-2 EA-6B det. In 1980 EA-6B-equipped VAQ-136 moved from Whidbey Island to Atsugi, replacing the VMAQ-2 det within CVW-5. The F/A-18A's introduction resulted in restructuring of CVW-5 between May and November 1986; three F/A-18A squadrons replaced CVW-5's two F-4S and two A-7E squadrons. VF-151 became VFA-151 at Lemoore on 1 June 1986, gaining F/A-18As before rejoining CVW-5 at Atsugi in November 1986. The same month F/A-18A-equipped VFA-192 and VFA-195 (both formerly LATWINGPAC A-7E Attack Squadrons at Lemoore) also joined CVW-5 at Atsugi. CVW-5's former VF-161 became VFA-161, transferring to LATWINGPAC at Lemoore in June 1986; VA-56 and VA-93 both disestablished on 31 August 1986. Additionally, VA-185 was established at Whidbey Island on 1 December 1986, moving to Atsugi during September 1987, joining VA-115 as a second A-6E/KA-6D CVW-5 squadron.

As well as HC-1 Det 2, a further HC-1 detachment was located aboard Atsugi: HC-1 Det 6 with one SH-3A, replaced by an SH-3G in 1981. HC-1 Det 6's SH-3s were VIP configured, supporting Commander of the Seventh Fleet (COMSEVENTHFLT), including aboard his flagship USS *Blue Ridge* (LCC-19).

As mentioned previously, Agana's VQ-1 maintained a regular EP-3 det aboard Atsugi.

HC-3 Det 105 with two CH-46s was aboard Atsugi until relocating to Agana during 1981.

Atsugi's station flight operated two C-117Ds and a UC-12B, a second UC-12B replacing one of the C-117Ds during 1980, with the other C-117D withdrawn during 1981. A third UC-12B was added during 1982.

CVW-5 aircraft on the deck of USS *Midway* (CV-41) on 17 May 1984, six days before the conclusion of her December 1983 to May 1984 WESTPAC/IO deployment. Visible aircraft include a HC-1 'Angels' Det.2 SH-3G, VAW-115 'Liberty Bells' E-2Bs, VF-151 'Vigilantes' and VF-161 'Chargers' F-4Ss, VA-56 'Champions' and VA-93 'Ravens' A-7Es, VA-115 'Eagles' A-6E TRAMs/KA-6Ds and VAQ-136 'Gauntlets' EA-6Bs. *Midway's* directly assigned COD C-1A is also just visible. Some of CVW-5's aircraft have received toned-down TPS camouflage. (NARA)

Above left: A VF-151 F-4S on the cat and about to launch from *Midway* on 1 March 1985. Live AIM-9L/Ms are visible underwing. *Midway* was conducting a short February–March 1985 WESTPAC deployment at this time. (NARA)

Above right: Crewmen wash VA-115 A-6E TRAMs on *Midway's* flight deck in the Sea of Japan at the conclusion of a September–October 1981 WESTPAC deployment. (NARA)

A VA-93 A-7E prepares to launch from *Midway* during the same 1981 deployment as the previous photograph. (NARA)

A HC-1 Det.2 SH-3G approaches to land on *Midway* on 2 December 1982, during Exercise Search and Rescue '82 off Hong Kong. This exercise also involved British and Hong Kong military and civilian participants as well as USAF assets. VA-115 A-6E TRAM and KA-6D, a VF-151 F-4S and a VA-93 A-7E are visible in the background. *Midway* was nearing the end of a September to December 1982 NORPAC/WESTPAC deployment. (NARA)

A VFA-192 'World Famous Golden Dragons' F/A-18A seen in June 1989, with a CATM-9L/M captive training Sidewinder on its port wing tip. (NARA)

North Island's HSL-33/HSL-35 and Barbers Point's HSL-37 maintained various SH-2F dets aboard Atsugi for shipboard deployments.

North Island's HC-11 operated HC-11 Det 9 aboard Atsugi during 1984–1985 and Agana's HC-5 operated HC-5 Det 4 aboard Atsugi during 1985; both operated two CH-46s. From 1985 onwards Cubi Point's VRC-50 operated a det (generally with two US-3As and four C-2As) aboard Atsugi, while Alameda's VR-55 and North Island's VR-57 both operated a C-9B det aboard Atsugi from the same year.

The USMC's MAG-36 (located at MCAS(H) Futenma, Okinawa) established two dets aboard Atsugi from 1985: HMH-361 Det (YN) with CH-53s and HMM-165 Det (YW) with CH-46s.

Cubi Point's VC-5 established a det with five A-4s aboard Atsugi during 1985.

Commander, Task Force 72 (CTF-72) controlled P-3s deployed to Atsugi and operating within the Seventh Fleet area under the PATWING ONE headquarters staff at NAVSUPPFA Kamiseya, Japan.

NAS Barbers Point, Hawaii

PATWING TWO was aboard Barbers Point, controlling VP-1 (YB) and VP-4 (YD), each with nine P-3Bs, and VP-6 (PC), VP-17 (ZE) and VP-22 (QA), each with nine P-3B TACNAVMODs in 1980. All operated P-3B TACNAVMODs by 1981. VP-4 transitioned to P-3Cs by 1984, VP-1 by 1985 and VP-17 by 1987; VP-6 and VP-22 retained P-3B TACNAVMODs for the remainder of the decade. PATWING TWO Patrol Squadrons made regular deployments to Adak, Agana and Cubi Point.

VP-4 operated a 'Special Project Detachment Barbers Point' (VP-4 SPECIAL PROJECT DET BARPT) with two P-3B TACNAVMODs conducting clandestine 'special projects'. This evolved into VPU-2 (also under PATWING TWO), which was established on 1 July 1982 as a counterpart to the AirLant's VPU-1, and like the latter made use of spurious BuNos and unit markings on its aircraft. VPU-2 operated two P-3B TACNAVMODs, joined by a UP-3A (used as a trainer) from 1985.

VC-1 (UA), under FITAEWWINGPAC control, provided adversary, target facilities, transport and utility support. It operated six TA-4Js, a VP-3A and a VC-118B in 1980. Two SH-3Gs were added during 1982. During 1983 the VC-118B was retired; a

Right: A VP-17 'White Lightnings' P-3B
in-flight off the coast of Waikiki. (NARA)

Below: A VP-17 P-3B investigates the Soviet
Kirov-class heavy nuclear-powered guided missile
cruiser *Frunze*, which was leading a Soviet Navy
surface action group in the Indian Ocean, on
1 October 1985. (NARA)

P-3A and a UH-3A were added. By 1986 VC-1 operated eight TA-4Js and two P-3As
whilst three CH-53As replaced the H-3s. From 1987 A-4Es joined VC-1, by 1988 the
squadron operated four TA-4Js, five A-4Es and three CH-53As.

HSL-37 (TH), under ASWWINGPAC, operated around eleven SH-2Fs for shipboard
deployment.

VQ-3 (TC) moved from FAIRWESTPAC control at Agana to PATWING TWO
control at Barbers Point during 1981 with two EC-130Qs and a KC-130F trainer/
support aircraft. By 1983 it built up to seven EC-130Qs, peaking at nine EC-130Qs,
usually with one or two KC-130Fs also assigned. On 3 August 1989 VQ-3 received the
first two E-6As, which would eventually replace the EC-130Q.

The Station Flight, under PATWINGSPAC control, operated a U-11A until 1983.
No aircraft were then assigned until 1987 when two P-3As joined the Station Flight.

A VC-1 'Blue Alii' TA-4J is prepared for flight at Barbers Point during Exercise Cope Canine '85 on 12 April 1985. (NARA)

Crewmen unload supplies from a VC-1 SH-3G in August 1984. (NARA)

Barbers Point routinely hosted many USN and USMC aircraft, as well as USAF and allied aircraft, deploying for exercises or other reasons. During 1985 the fixed-wing USMC squadrons of MAG-24 temporarily relocated to Barbers Point due to the closure of the runways at their home station, MCAS Kaneohe Bay, Hawaii; VMFA-212 (WD) and VMFA-235 (DB), each with twelve F-4S (MAG-24's other F-4S squadron, VMFA-232, was on deployment to MCAS Iwakuni, Japan), along with the four TA-4Fs of Headquarters and Maintenance Squadron H&MS-24 (EW).

NAS Cubi Point, Republic of the Philippines

Cubi Point's FAIRWESTPAC squadrons were VC-5 (UE) and VRC-50 (RG). VC-5 conducted adversary/target towing support with A-4s, drone operations with MQM/BQM-74Cs and BQM-34Ss, provided surface target boats with QST-33/35s and operated helicopters for drone recovery, general support and insertion of Marine, SEAL or rescue ground forces. From 1980 VC-5 operated nine A-4Es, three TA-4Js and two SH-3Gs. During 1985 VC-5's SH-3G fleet peaked at seven and three CH-53Es were added. By 1988 the CH-53Es were gone, VC-5 operating eleven A-4Es, three TA-4Js and five SH-3G. An A-4E was lost in a fatal crash during a training flight on 19 July 1989.

VC-5 'Checkertails' A-4Es and a TA-4J on the Cubi Point flight line during 1981. An NC-8A Mobile Electric Power Plant (MEPP) is in the foreground. (NARA)

A VC-5 SH-3G crewman attaching a recovery sling to a BQM-34S Firebee target drone, which is floating in the ocean after use, near to Wallace Air Station, Poro Point, San Fernando, Philippines, from where it had been launched. (NARA)

VRC-50 operated five C-1As, seven C-2As, two CT-39Es and three C-130Fs in 1980. To support WESTPAC/IO COD duties, a number of (mostly pre-production) S-3As were converted into US-3As; their long-range (which could be further extended via air-to-air refuelling) and relatively high speed particularly suited them to use in the region with VRC-50, which they joined from 1982. VRC-50 eventually built up to six US-3As, when the sole KS-3A (latterly operated by VS-41) was converted into a US-3A in 1985 and reassigned to VRC-50; as noted previously, it was lost in a fatal crash with VRC-50 on 20 January 1989. The C-1A fleet had increased to six by 1981, but were withdrawn by 1982. By 1988 only a single CT-39E remained, and that was soon withdrawn. In late 1989 five US-3As, eight C-2As and three C-130Fs were operated.

In 1980 the Station Flight (8B), under FAIRWESTPAC control, operated four HH-46As (withdrawn by 1984), one UC-12B (increased to two later that year) and three C-117Ds (which were withdrawn by 1982). By 1986 only a single UC-12B remained; this was joined by two UC-12Fs by 1988.

HSL-31 maintained a det aboard Cubi Point until 1981, as did VQ-1 with an EP-3E and an EA-3B (just EP-3Es following the late 1988 withdrawal of EA-3Bs). There was also a rotationally deployed P-3 squadron, and regular dets from CVWs and by USMC tactical aircraft.

Left: A VRC-50 'Foo Dogs' US-3A about to be launched from USS *Carl Vinson* in the North Pacific on 21 January 1987. (NARA)

Below: One of two Cubi Point station flight UC-12Bs on the flight line during May 1981. (NARA)

NAVSUPPFA/NAF Diego Garcia

NAF Diego Garcia was commissioned in 1981, within Naval Support Facility Diego Garcia, on the tiny, but strategically important, British Indian Ocean Territory island of the same name. In 1987 the NAF decommissioned, with the airfield facilities (which were also expanded to host USAF deployments that year) subsequently returning to direct NAVSUPPFA Diego Garcia control. Tensions with Iran increased Diego Garcia's importance, resulting in its ongoing development to support expanding USN IO operations.

From 1983 HC-1 Det 3 (previously assigned to CVW-14 aboard *Coral Sea* until 1982) operated two SH-3Gs aboard Diego Garcia; in 1984 the base flight absorbed these support duties and subsequently operated the two SH-3Gs under COMFAIRWESTPAC control until 1987.

VP and VS squadrons made rotational P-3 and S-3 dets aboard Diego Garcia. In 1983 NAVSUPPFA Kamiseya's PATWING ONE established PATWING ONE Det Diego Garcia to oversee these operations. From 1984 these VP/VS partial-squadron dets were replaced by rotational VP full-squadron P-3 deployments.

VQ-1 also operated a rotational EP-3E/EA-3B det aboard Diego Garcia.

From 1982 VRC-50 COD US-3As were detached aboard Diego Garcia whenever US aircraft carriers were operating in the IO.

NAF Kadena, Okinawa. Japan

COMFLEACTS (Commander Fleet Activities) Okinawa/NAF Kadena, hosted within the USAF's Kadena Air Base (AB), primarily supported P-3C deployments. For much of the decade full PATWING TWO/TEN VP squadrons of nine P-3Cs deployed rotationally. By the end of the decade full Patrol Squadrons no longer deployed, but continuous P-3C detachments from Moffett Field and Misawa were supported (three to six P-3Cs supported daily).

Until 1983 Kadena supported a rotational USMC AV-8A det of around six aircraft.

COMFLTACT Okinawa (8H) operated a C-117D, replaced by a UC-12B during 1981. Until 1983 1st MAW (Marine Liaison Office) also operated a CT-39 aboard Kadena.

Kadena routinely supported transient naval aircraft, particularly USMC tactical aircraft from MCAS Iwakuni (A-4s, A-6s, F-4s and F/A-18s) and helicopters/OV-10s from MCAS Futenma, Okinawa. Other typical transient aircraft came from CVW-5, VC-5, VRC-50 and VQ-1 amongst many other units.

NAF Midway Island

Located on Midway Atoll's remote Sand Island, with no based aviation units, this primarily served as a trans-Pacific refuelling stop. After being downgraded from NAS to NAF in 1978, no permanent military personnel were assigned, personnel were instead temporarily rotated.

NAF Misawa, Japan

Hosted within the USAF's Misawa AB, this primarily supported rotational full VP/P-3C squadron deployments from PATWING TWO/TEN under PATWINGONE control.

The station flight operated C-1As, fluctuating between three and four, one being permanently forward deployed to Seoul for logistic support by Commander, Naval Forces Korea (COMNAVFORKOREA). The C-1As were withdrawn by 1986; after a hiatus, a UC-12B was received during November 1986 (adopting 8M identification code).

Misawa regularly supported CVW-5 and VQ-1 dets and USMC dets from MCAS Iwakuni (MAG-12 VMA squadrons/MAG-15 VMFA squadrons).

A VP-50 P-3C seen while deployed to Misawa from Moffett Field during 1984. (NARA)

Carriers and Carrier Air Wings

Carriers

The oldest operational USN aircraft carriers during the 1980s were the 'Midway' class, USS *Midway* (CV-41) and USS *Coral Sea* (CV-43), both laid down during the Second World War and periodically updated to allow for operation of modern aircraft.

The first supercarriers were the 'Forrestal' class, USS *Forrestal* (CV-59), USS *Saratoga* (CV-60), USS *Ranger* (CV-61) and USS *Independence* (CV-62). These were followed by the improved 'Kitty Hawk' class: USS *Kitty Hawk* (CV-63), USS *Constellation* (CV-64), USS *America* (CV-66) and USS *John F. Kennedy* (CV-67). *America* and *Kennedy* were originally intended to be nuclear-powered, before reverting to conventional propulsion; they differed considerably not only to *Kitty Hawk/Constellation*, but also to each other. To extend the life of these classes during the 1980s, many underwent the Service Life Extension Program (SLEP), a complex twenty-eight-month modernisation programme which added ten to fifteen years of service life.

The unique USS *Enterprise* (CVN-65) was the first nuclear-powered supercarrier.

The definitive Cold War nuclear supercarrier design was the 'Nimitz' class, USS *Nimitz* (CVN-68), USS *Dwight D. Eisenhower* (CVN-69), USS *Carl Vinson* (CVN-70), USS *Theodore Roosevelt* (CVN-71) and USS *Abraham Lincoln* (CVN-72). *Abraham Lincoln* was the last 'Nimitz' class supercarrier to commission during the 1980s (being commissioned on 11 November 1989, although not becoming operational until 1990,

USS *Midway*, lead-ship of her class, anchored in its home port, Yokosuka, Japan, at the conclusion of a December 1983 to May 1984 WESTPAC/ IO deployment. CVW-5 aircraft are visible on deck. (NARA)

making her first deployment in 1991). However, further 'Nimitz' class supercarriers would be constructed in the following decades, replacing the earlier classes.

One further carrier was in USN service, the USS *Lexington* (AVT-16) of the old 'Essex' class, used exclusively as an aviation training carrier, homeported at Pensacola.

USS *Saratoga*, of the 'Forrestal' class, tied up at pier at Diego Garcia on 16 December 1985. This was the first time an aircraft carrier had visited the island. CVW-17 aircraft are seen on *Saratoga's* deck. *Saratoga* was conducting an August 1985 to April 1986 deployment that would also see her conduct operations off Libya. (NARA)

USS *Constellation*, of the 'Kitty Hawk' class, seen underway in the Pacific on 16 December 1988, in the early stages of a December 1988 to June 1989 WESTPAC/ IO deployment. CVW-14 aircraft are on deck. (NARA)

USS *Dwight D. Eisenhower*, of the 'Nimitz' class, is overflown by a formation of VA-72 A-7Es on 1 August 1988, at the conclusion of Ike's February to August 1988 Mediterranean deployment. Other CVW-7 aircraft can be seen on deck. (NARA)

Atlantic Fleet Carrier Assignments

USS *Coral Sea* (CV-43) homeported at Norfolk after transferring from PACFLT during 1983.

USS *Forrestal* (CV-59) homeported at Mayport (underwent SLEP at Philadelphia January 1983–May 1985).

USS *Saratoga* (CV-60) homeported at Mayport (SLEP at Philadelphia September 1980–May 1983).

USS *Independence* (CV-62) homeported at Norfolk (SLEP at Philadelphia February 1985–June 1988, *Independence* was subsequently reassigned to PACFLT).

USS *Kitty Hawk* (CV-63) temporarily transferred from PACFLT to LANTFLT in 1987 for SLEP at Philadelphia, rejoining PACFLT after completing SLEP in 1990.

USS *America* (CV-66) homeported at Norfolk.

USS *John F. Kennedy* (CV-67) homeported at Norfolk.

USS *Nimitz* (CVN-68) homeported at Norfolk – transferred to PACFLT in 1987.

USS *Dwight D. Eisenhower* (CVN-69) homeported at Norfolk.

USS *Carl Vinson* (CVN-70) briefly assigned to LANTFLT following commissioning on 13 March 1982, departing Norfolk on 1 March 1983 for her maiden deployment, an eight-month, around-the-world cruise, concluding on 28 October 1983 at her new PACFLT homeport, Alameda.

USS *Theodore Roosevelt* (CVN-71) homeported at Norfolk, after commissioning 25 October 1986.

Pacific Fleet Carrier Assignments

USS *Midway* (CV-41) homeported at Yokosuka, Japan.

USS *Coral Sea* (CV-43) homeported at Alameda. Transferring to the LANTFLT in 1983, leaving Alameda on 25 March for a six-month, around-the-world cruise, which concluded at her new homeport, Norfolk.

USS *Ranger* (CV-61) homeported at San Diego.

USS *Independence* (CV-62) transferred to PACFLT in 1988, arriving at her new homeport, San Diego, on 8 October.

USS *Kitty Hawk* (CV-63) homeported at San Diego, until departing there on 3 January 1987 for temporary assignment to LANTFLT for SLEP.

USS *Constellation* (CV-64) homeported at San Diego.

USS *Enterprise* (CVN-65) homeported at Alameda.

USS *Nimitz* (CVN-68) transferred to PACFLT in 1987, arriving at her new homeport, Bremerton, Washington, on 2 July 1987.

USS *Carl Vinson* (CVN-70) transferred to PACFLT after brief assignment to LANTFLT, arriving at her new homeport, Alameda, on 28 October 1983, where she replaced *Coral Sea* with PACFLT.

Carrier Air Wings (CVWs)

Most 1980s supercarrier CVWs consisted of the following squadrons: two VF (F-4/F-14); two light VA (A-7), transitioning during the decade to two VFA (F/A-18);

a medium VA (A-6/KA-6); a VAW (E-2); a VAQ (EA-6B); a VS (S-3); and a HS (SH-3). Sometimes USMC squadrons were assigned, in lieu of USN squadrons. Other temporary detachments were often made to CVWs: VQ (EA-3B), VFP (RF-8G) and VRC (C-1A/C-2A/US-3A) squadron dets.

Squadrons going to sea with CVWs did not always deploy with all their assigned aircraft. For example, while VF, light VA and VFA squadrons generally had twelve aircraft, flight-/hangar-deck space on the assigned carrier (which varied) might dictate that squadrons left two or three aircraft ashore when deploying.

As well as their assigned, unique, six-digit BuNo aircraft identity serial, naval aircraft also had a separate 'MODEX' number, usually applied to the aircraft in larger digits than the BuNo. For squadrons assigned to CVWs, different squadron types were assigned different three-digit MODEX ranges. Generally, the two F-4/F-14 squadrons received '1xx'/'2xx' range MODEXes, the two A-7 or F/A-18 squadrons '3xx'/'4xx', the A-6/KA-6 squadron '5xx', the E-2 squadron '600-603', the EA-6B squadron '604-607' and/or '62x', the SH-3 squadron '610-617', and the S-3 squadron '7xx'. The MODEX was used in conjunction with the two-letter unit identification code (see below) as part of the aircraft's unique identification radar 'squawk' transponder codes; as this is an octal-based system, MODEXes could only use digits 0–7, and not 8/9.

While most naval aviation squadrons had an assigned two-letter (or, for station flights, a letter/number) identification code, CVWs had their own assigned two-letter identification code (in the 'Ax' range for AirLant CVWs, 'Nx' range for AirPac CVWs); assigned squadrons used the identification code of their CVW, rather than each having their own squadron identification code. Aircraft temporarily attached to the CVW generally retained their own squadron identification code, although EA-3Bs occasionally adopted the CVW's identification code when attached.

John Lehman, Secretary of the Navy 1981–1987, himself a naval reserve A-6 B/N, was a major A-6 proponent. One of Lehman's goals was to increase the A-6 squadrons per CVW to two, while retaining the two F-14/VF and two F/A-18/VFA squadrons and other supporting squadrons, forming the 'Notional air wing'. Only CVW-8/*Theodore Roosevelt* became so-equipped, from 1988; the two A-6 Squadrons, VA-35 and VA-36, adopted '5xx' and '53x' MODEXes, operating only A-6Es, without KA-6Ds. Two other CVWs (CVW-2/*Ranger* from 1986 and CVW-3/*John F. Kennedy* from 1983) adopted an experimental 'All-Grumman' air wing, so called as, apart from the S-3/ SH-3 squadrons, its squadrons were all equipped with Grumman F-14s (24) and A-6s (24-28), as well as EA-6Bs and E-2s, while lacking LTV A-7/McDonnell Douglas F/A-18 squadrons.

The smaller Midway-class had adapted CVWs; F/A-18s replaced F-4s as these smaller carriers were unable to safely operate F-14s. CVW-5/*Midway* initially operated a fairly standard arrangement: two F-4, two A-7, one A-6E/KA-6D, one E-2B and one EA-6B squadrons, supported by SH-3G/USMC RF-4B dets. From July 1984 an SH-3H squadron replaced the SH-3G det, and the RF-4B det no longer deployed. From 1986 CVW-5 had three F/A-18 squadrons, along with one each A-6E/KA-6D, E-2, EA-6B and SH-3H; from September 1987 a second A-6E/KA-6D squadron was added. CVW-14/ *Coral Sea* initially operated a similar arrangement to *Midway*, with two F-4, two A-7, one A-6E/KA-6D and one E-2 squadrons (no EA-6B squadron), supported by RF-8G/ SH-3G dets. After *Coral Sea* transferred from PACFLT to LANTFLT, CVW-13 was assigned. For the first *Coral Sea*/CVW-13 cruise in 1985, it had four F/A-18 squadrons and one each A-6E/KA-6D, E-2C, SH-3H and EA-6B; from 1987 it operated three

USS *Kitty Hawk's* assigned COD C-1A lands aboard on 24 February 1983. Such COD aircraft were individually directly assigned to carriers (rather than to the CVW assigned to the carrier) until the mid-/late 1980s. (NARA)

F/A-18 squadrons, two A-6E squadrons (only one with KA-6Ds) and one each E-2C, SH-3H and EA-6B.

Until the mid/late 1980s, carriers (including *Lexington*) routinely had individual COD C-1As directly assigned, separate to their CVW. The last of these, and also the USN's last operational reciprocating-engine aircraft, was *Lexington's* C-1A BuNo 146048. It made its final trap aboard *Lexington* on 27 September 1988 and retired on 30 September.

Atlantic Fleet CVWs

CVW-1 (AB)
Conducted its final deployment aboard *John F. Kennedy* August 1980–March 1981; reassigned to *America* for the remainder of the decade. CVW-1 also deployed aboard *Theodore Roosevelt* during a January–February 1987 shakedown cruise to Guantanamo Bay.

A formation of CVW-1 aircraft overfly USS *America* while she was underway in the Indian Ocean on 21 April 1983, during a December 1982 to June 1983 Mediterranean/IO deployment. VF-33 and VF-102 F-14As lead VA-46 and VA-72 A-7Es, VA-34 A-6Es and VS-32 S-3As. Other units assigned to CVW-1 at this time were VAW-123 (E-2Cs), VAQ-136 (EA-6Bs – although VAQ-136 only joined CVW-1 aboard *America* from 6 February 1983 onwards), HS-11 (SH-3Hs), plus dets from VQ-2 (EA-3B) and VRC-50 (C-2A), the latter also only aboard from February 1983. (NARA)

CVW-3 (AC)
Conducted its final cruise aboard *Saratoga* March–August 1980; reassigned to *John F. Kennedy* for the remainder of the decade.

CVW-6 (AE)
Assigned to *Independence*; reassigned to *Forrestal* in 1985.

CVW-7 (AG)
Assigned to *Dwight D. Eisenhower* throughout.

CVW-8 (AJ)
Assigned to *Nimitz*; reassigned to *Theodore Roosevelt* in 1988. CVW-8 also deployed aboard *Carl Vinson* during an April–June 1982 shakedown Caribbean cruise.

CVW-13 (AK)
Established 1 March 1984, assigned to *Coral Sea*.

CVW-17 (AA)
Assigned to *Forrestal*; reassigned to *Saratoga* in 1984. Conducted a one-off deployment with *Independence*, for her Norfolk to San Diego cruise as she transferred to PACFLT August–October 1988.

CVWR-20 (AF)
This Reserve Air Wing made Western Atlantic (WESTLANT) training deployments as a full air wing aboard *Carl Vinson* July 1982, *Dwight D. Eisenhower* June–July 1984 and July–August 1989, and *Forrestal* June 1987.

Pacific Fleet CVWs

CVW-2 (NE)
Assigned to *Ranger* throughout the decade; CVW-2 also conducted a single WESTPAC/ IO cruise aboard *Kitty Hawk* January–August 1984.

CVW-5 (NF)
Assigned to *Midway* throughout.

CVW-9 (NG)
Assigned to *Constellation*, subsequently conducting a single deployment aboard *Ranger* July 1983–February 1984, and two deployments aboard *Kitty Hawk* July–December 1985 and January–June 1987 (the latter a world cruise, San Diego to Norfolk, as *Kitty Hawk* temporarily transferred to LANTFLT for SLEP). Reassigned to *Nimitz* from 1988.

CVW-10 (NM)
Briefly existed 1 November 1986–30 September 1988, never receiving a full complement of squadrons. Originally intended for assignment to *Abraham Lincoln*; its only sea deployment saw elements deploy aboard *Enterprise* July–August 1987 for CARQUALS before it was decided to disestablish CVW-10.

A formation of CVW-9 aircraft overfly USS *Kitty Hawk*, as part of an air power demonstration on 28 June 1986, during a dependant's day cruise between CVW-9's two operational deployments aboard *Kitty Hawk*. VF-24 and VF-211 F-14As lead VA-146 and VA-147 A-7Es, VA-165 A-6Es/KA-6Ds and VS-33 S-3As. Also assigned to CVW-9 at this time was VAW-112 (E-2Cs), VAQ-130 (EA-6Bs) and HS-2 (SH-3Hs). (NARA)

CVW-11 (NH)
PACFLT's CVW-11 had uniquely been deploying with LANTFLT's *America* since 1979, conducting its final *America* deployment April–November 1981. Reassigned to *Enterprise* for the remainder of the decade.

CVW-14 (NK)
Assigned to *Coral Sea*. Conducted its final *Coral Sea* deployment March–September 1983 for a world cruise, Alameda to Norfolk, via the Suez Canal, as *Coral Sea* transferred to LANTFLT. Subsequently reassigned to *Constellation*.

CVW-15 (NL)
Assigned to *Kitty Hawk*; reassigned to *Carl Vinson*, first deploying with her March–October 1983 for a Norfolk to Alameda world cruise as she transferred to PACFLT.

CVWR-30 (ND)
This Reserve Air Wing made EASTPAC training deployments as a full air wing aboard *Coral Sea* March 1981, *Ranger* January–February 1986, and *Enterprise* August 1988.

Naval Aviation in Combat

During the 1980s the intended wartime mission of multiple LANTFLT CVBGs was to attack targets around the Kola Peninsula in the Soviet north-west. Meanwhile several PACFLT CVBGs would strike targets in the Soviet Far East. These battles would take place remote from other NATO or Allied assets, with the CVBGs fighting in isolation. F-14s, remaining F-4s and new F/A-18s would defend the CVBGs and escort strike packages, while E-2s managed the air battle, also feeding their radar picture directly to the Tactical Information Display in the F-14's rear cockpit. A-6s, A-7s and F/A-18s would strike land and sea targets, and conduct *Iron Hand* (Suppression of Enemy Air Defences – SEAD) missions. All A-6s and A-7s could carry AGM-45 Shrike anti-radiation missiles (ARMs). Ten A-6Es were equipped with the AN/AWG-21 system, allowing them to carry the AGM-78 Standard ARM ('STARM'), split between AirLant (which usually sent two or three out with deploying squadrons), and AirPac (all concentrated within VA-115 in Japan). In 1980 these were replaced by eight similarly modified A-6E TRAMs (AirPac's examples transferred from VA-115 to VA-145 in 1986). In 1988 the STARMs were withdrawn. AGM-88 High-speed ARMs (HARMs) were introduced from 1985 with A-7s and F/A-18s. EA-6Bs provided electronic countermeasures (ECM) support, later gaining HARM compatibility. RF-8Gs, and ultimately F-14As (or USMC RF-4Bs for CVW-5 until 1984), conducted tactical reconnaissance. KA-6Ds, and 'buddy-pack' equipped A-6s and A-7s, provided tanker support. S-3s provided ASW coverage, augmented closer-in to the CVBG by SH-3s, the latter also providing search and rescue support, both 'plane guard' during carrier flight operations as well as further afield.

Fortunately the Cold War never turned hot. However, U.S. naval aviation saw plenty of action during the 1980s.

As 1980 dawned, America was already faced with the Iran hostage crisis; following the Islamic Revolution, Iranian students stormed the U.S. Embassy in Tehran on 4 November 1979, taking sixty-six American diplomats and citizens hostage. *Midway* arrived on station in the Indian Ocean on 18 November 1979, followed in turn by *Kitty Hawk*, *Nimitz*, *Coral Sea*, *Dwight D. Eisenhower* and *Independence*. A rescue attempt, Operation *Eagle Claw*, was planned for April 1980. *Nimitz*/CVW-8 and *Coral Sea*/CVW-14 were then on station ready to provide support, their combat aircraft marked with wingtip identification stripes. Integral to the plan were HM-16 RH-53Ds; initially six deployed aboard *Kitty Hawk* from 28 November 1979, before moving to *Nimitz* (joining a further two already aboard) upon the latter's arrival on station in January 1980. While USAF HH-53s or USMC CH-53s may have been better suited to the mission, RH-53Ds were chosen as a security precaution; their presence in the region could be explained by their usual mine-countermeasures duties. During the planning, to allow more appropriate air crew to operate the eight RH-53Ds, all except

Ahead of Operation *Eagle Claw*, six HM-16 'Seahawks' RH-53Ds, still in their usual Engine Gray paint scheme, in formation over USS *Nimitz* soon after they moved from *Kitty Hawk* to *Nimitz*. A seventh RH-53D is on deck, along with CVW-8 aircraft. *Nimitz* was conducting a September 1979 to May 1980 Mediterranean/IO/Arabian Sea deployment, and she relieved *Kitty Hawk* off Iran during January 1980. (NARA)

F-14As of VF-41 'Black Aces' and VF-84 'Jolly Rogers' aboard *Nimitz* soon before Operation *Eagle Claw* was launched. They have received special identification markings on their starboard wings for the operation; black and red stripes for VF-41, and black and yellow stripes for VF-84. They are armed with live AIM-7s under the fuselage and live AIM-9s under the wings. (NARA)

three of the USN air crew were replaced by twelve USMC, and one USAF, pilots and co-pilots; the RH-53D variant was unfamiliar to these CH/HH-53 pilots.

The complex rescue plan involved three USAF MC-130Es carrying a 118-man Delta Force assault team to the 'Desert One' forward staging area in the Iranian desert, joined by three USAF EC-130Es, acting as ground tankers with bladder fuel tanks in the hold. There the MC/EC-130s would be met by the RH-53Ds flying in from *Nimitz*. Once refuelled and loaded with the Delta personnel, the RH-53Ds would move the assault force to the 'Desert Two' hide site, nearer Tehran. Delta would subsequently approach the embassy via ground transport and launch the assault; the RH-53Ds would then extract them and the rescued hostages, conveying them to an Iranian airfield, secured by U.S. Army Rangers, where USAF C-141s would fly them out of Iran.

Operation *Eagle Claw* was launched on 24 April 1980. Of the eight RH-53Ds (Bluebeard 1 to 8) flying into Iran, Bluebeard 6 suffered a mechanical problem and landed in the Iranian desert, its crew picked up by Bluebeard 8. Bluebeard 6's USMC pilot, being unfamiliar with the RH-53D, had assumed that the warning light indicated that a blade failure was imminent, as it would have in his usual CH-53; in fact a newer system aboard the RH-53D did not mean that such a failure was imminent. The remaining RH-53Ds proceeded through two unexpected 'haboob' dust storms, bringing crews zero visibility, unbearably high temperatures and choking dust. Bluebeard 5, experiencing technical problems and struggling in the haboob, turned back for *Nimitz*. The six remaining RH-53Ds proceeded to Desert One. First to arrive, Bluebeard 3 landed hard, damaging its undercarriage. Bluebeard 2 was experiencing hydraulic problems, and soon after arriving it was decided it could not continue; this only left five RH-53Ds, one less than the minimum required for the operation to proceed; the mission was therefore aborted. After the remaining RH-53Ds refuelled they had to make way for the EC-130Es, now low on fuel, to take off first. Bluebeard 3, unable to taxi due to its damaged undercarriage, had to leapfrog over EC-130E Republic 4; disorientated in the swirling dust, Bluebeard 3 struck Republic 4's tail, crashing down on the EC-130E, tragically killing three aboard Bluebeard 3 and five aboard Republic 4. It was quickly decided to abandon the remaining helicopters and there was a chaotic scramble as personnel boarded the three MC-130Es and two remaining EC-130Es for evacuation. The abandoned RH-53Ds were subsequently absorbed into Islamic Republic of Iran Navy service, joining six previously acquired by the Shah. Despite planning a second rescue attempt, the remaining fifty-two hostages were eventually released by Iran on 20 January 1981, after 444 days captivity. The disastrous Operation *Eagle Claw* would directly result in restructuring of U.S. Special Forces, and creation of the multi-service United States Special Operations Command.

As well as Iran, a number of Arab nations were beginning to cause America increasing concern, specifically Libya and Syria.

Libya's Colonel Gaddafi not only sponsored international terrorist groups, but also claimed the Gulf of Sidra as Libyan territorial waters, declaring a 'Line of Death' across the Gulf's northern boundary, with Libyan interceptors patrolling the area. The U.S.A. considered these international waters, and diplomatically protested the Libyan

Tow tractors position two of the HM-16 RH-53Ds aboard *Nimitz* prior to the launch of Operation *Eagle Claw*. They have been repainted in overall FS30279 Desert Sand, and have also had their Engine Air Particle Separators (EAPS) removed. EAPS, usually fitted to the front of the T64 engines, eliminated ingestion of dust and foreign objects. However, their removal would improve airflow into the engine, resulting in increased power, improved fuel economy and therefore longer range. Nonetheless, bearing in mind the haboob dust storms that the helicopters would encounter, the crews may have been glad to have retained the EAPS. (NARA)

stance from 1974, but did little more. However, under President Reagan, USN ships began conducting freedom of navigation (FON) exercises in the Gulf of Sidra.

After two Libyan Arab Republic Air Force (LARAF) MiG-25PDs (unsuccessfully) fired upon a USAF RC-135 on 16 September 1980, a further RC-135 mission on 21 September was escorted by three F-14As from *John F. Kennedy*/CVW-1; five LARAF Mirage 5s intercepted but were seen off by the F-14As without opening fire.

On 1 August 1981 the FON received President Reagan's authorisation; new Rules of Engagement (ROE), known as 'Reagan ROE', allowed on-scene commanders more latitude to authorise use of force. Two CVBGs, centred on *Forrestal*/CVW-17 and *Nimitz*/CVW-8, moved into position north of the Gulf of Sidra on 18 August, to commence the FON and Open Ocean Missile Exercise (OOMEX). CVW-8 F-14As and CVW-17 F-4Js were placed on Barrier Combat Air Patrol (BARCAP) between the fleet and Libya, with the southernmost F-14As patrolling to the south of the so-called Line of Death; soon two USN destroyers crossed the Line of Death. The LARAF immediately responded with seventy combat aircraft, both interceptors (MiG-23MS, MiG-25PD, Mirage F.1s) and attack/reconnaissance types (Su-22/22M, MiG-25RBK), which engaged the USN BARCAPs, especially the south-western F-14A BARCAPS. However, E-2C control, and support from EA-6Bs and land-based EP-3s (jamming LARAF aircraft radars and communications) meant that the USN interceptors were able to enter each engagement from a favourable position, behind the LARAF aircraft, forcing the latter's withdrawal. However, on three occasions LARAF aircraft penetrated the exercise area, causing temporary suspension of the OOMEX.

The following morning, 19 August, two VF-41 F-14As patrolled the southern BARCAP: VF-41 CO, Commander Henry 'Hank' Kleeman, with radar intercept officer (RIO) Lt David 'DJ' Venlet in Fast Eagle 102 (BuNo 160403/'AJ-102'), and Lt Lawrence 'Music' Muczynski with RIO Lt JG James 'Amos' Anderson in Fast Eagle 107 (BuNo 160390/'AJ-107'). After refuelling from a VA-35 KA-6D, they established their 'race-track' pattern, one of the pair always heading on the threat axis. Suddenly, a fast contact was simultaneously detected heading towards them by the threat-facing F-14A and a VAW-124 E-2C. As the F-14As headed towards the target, they sidestepped for lateral separation, so that they could turn behind at the merge. However, the contact turned into each jink that the F-14As performed. Now heading straight for the contact, the F-14As accelerated to 550 kts (1,000 km/h). At around 8 miles (13 km) the contact was identified as two Su-22M 'Fitter-Js' in 'welded wing' formation (within 150 feet of each other). At the merge, the lead LARAF Su-22M pilot radioed his wingman to announce he had fired an AAM (as recorded by US ELINT/SIGINT aircraft in the area). Launched outside parameters, the Libyan AAM did not guide on its target, passing under Kleeman/Venlet; Muczynski/Anderson were positioned higher, looking down on the Su-22Ms. Observing the AAM launch, Kleeman ordered Muczynski to take the lead Su-22M, while he went after the wingman. The F-14s performed brake turns, pumping out chaff and flares as they did so, manoeuvring on to the Su-22M's tails. The Su-22M pilots failed to throw the F-14As off their tails; with the ROE satisfied, the F-14As each dispatched 'their' Su-22M with a single AIM-9L. There were further attempted engagements throughout the day, but no more shots fired; the OOMEX concluded later that day.

The U.S.A., France, Italy and the United Kingdom contributed to the peacekeeping Multinational Force (MNF) in Lebanon, intended to stabilise Lebanon and oversee the withdrawal of foreign forces (Israeli, Syrian and Palestine Liberation Organization) from Lebanon. The U.S. contributed Marines, who arrived on 25 August 1982; once PLO forces were evacuated, the MNF withdrew on 9 September. However, Lebanese President-elect

Gemayel's 14 September assassination resulted in a rapidly deteriorating security situation and increased Israeli intervention; a new MNF was rapidly dispatched, entering Beirut on 29 September. The US contingent was again primarily USMC, including CH-46s, CH-53s and UH-1Ns. Progressively drawn into a quagmire, with several factions ceasing to view it as a neutral force, the MNF increasingly became a target. The darkest hour came with the simultaneous suicide truck bombings of the U.S. and French barracks in Beirut on 23 October 1983, killing 241 U.S. servicemen and fifty-eight French paratroopers.

On 3 December 1983, Syrian SAMs targeted TARPS-equipped VF-32 F-14As near Beirut; *John F. Kennedy*/CVW-3 and *Independence*/CVW-6 on 'Bagel Station' east of Cyprus launched a disastrous Alpha strike in response on 4 December. Aircraft hastily launched, mostly loaded with inappropriate or insufficient ordnance, and with improperly briefed crews. The Syrian positions around Beirut were attacked, in daylight and without *Iron Hand* SEAD support, by six VA-15/VA-87 (Independence/CVW-6)

Two HMM-162 'Golden Eagles' CH-46Es at Beirut International Airport while supporting the MNF during April 1983. (NARA)

U.S. Marines load mail from a truck into a CH-53E at Beirut International Airport during April 1983, while supporting the MNF. This CH-53E is attached to HMM-162 (a CH-46E squadron). It was usual practice, when various helicopter types (or AV-8 Harriers), from multiple squadrons, deployed to sea together on amphibious assault ships, for one squadron to take control of all the multiple types deployed. The squadron would then have the suffix '(REINFORCED)' added to the unit designation for the duration. If the lead squadron left some of its own aircraft behind at the home station when deploying, but was also reinforced with other types from other squadrons during the deployment, the dual suffixes '(-)(REINFORCED)' were added. (NARA)

A-7Es and seventeen A-6Es (*Kennedy*/CVW-3 contributing seven from VA-85 and five from VA-75; Independence/CVW-6 contributing five from VA-176). One VA-85 A-6E (and the only fully loaded one) was shot down by a SAM, with pilot Lt Mark Lange killed and B/N Lt Bobby Goodman captured by Syrian forces. A VA-15 A-7E, flown by Cdr Ed 'Hunyak' Andrews (CVW-6's commander, or 'CAG'), and which had taken over as on-scene SAR commander for the downed A-6, was also hit by a SAM and shot down; Andrews was subsequently recovered. Another VA-15 A-7E was hit but recovered to the carrier. The bombing results were subsequently assessed as 'effective'; professionally, however, the strike was viewed as disastrous. As noted previously, one of the results of this debacle was the establishment of 'Strike-U' in October 1984.

On 1 September 1983, a Soviet Su-15 shot down Korean Air Lines Flight 007, a Boeing 747-230B, west of Sakhalin Island, killing all 269 aboard, including sixty-one Americans, after it strayed into Soviet air space. Subsequent operations were tense, with Soviet and U.S. forces in close proximity. VP-40's P-3Cs, deployed to Misawa at the time, participated in the USAF-led SAR/salvage operations, frequently encountering Soviet fighters.

Operation *Urgent Fury*, the U.S. invasion of Grenada, launched on 25 October 1983, alongside six allied Caribbean nations. It was undertaken due to instability resulting from rivalry within Grenada's communist leadership, and concerns for the safety of U.S. medical students on the island. Intervention would also remove Grenada's Cuban presence, and prevent a possible future Soviet presence there. USMC helicopters from USS *Guam* (LPH-9) supported the invasion force. Independence/CVW-6 had departed Norfolk on 18 October 1983 for the Mediterranean to relieve *Eisenhower* on Bagel Station for Lebanon operations. However, on 23 October 1983 (the day of the Beirut suicide bombings) *Independence* detoured to the Caribbean to support *Urgent Fury*. Army Rangers parachuted onto Point Salines Airport early on 25 October, meeting stiff opposition from Cuban and Grenadian soldiers; four VA-87 A-7Es provided close air support (CAS), with Mk 82 500 lb bombs, CBU-59 Anti-Personnel/Anti-Material (APAM) cluster bomb units (CBUs) and strafing runs. Soon after, two USMC AH-1Ts were shot down by anti-aircraft (AA) guns, with three of the four crewmembers killed; VA-15/VA-87 A-7Es strafed the AA positions. A-6Es (VA-176) and A-7Es provided ongoing support throughout the operation; on 27 October eight A-7Es (four from each squadron) struck Calivigny barracks in *Urgent Fury's* last major air attack. Communications problems arose during the operation; the USN/USMC used UHF radios, while the US Army used VHF, complicating communications between the latter and USN aircraft providing CAS.

Four HM-14 RH-53Ds (including one airframe borrowed from HM-12) conducted twenty-two consecutive days of minehunting operations in the Red Sea from 17 August 1984 during Operation *Intense Look*, after a Libyan ferry (with Libyan Navy crew) laid mines there. A HC-4 CH-53E later reinforced them. HM-14's main body operated from USS *Shreveport* (LPD-12), while Det One operated out of Jeddah, Saudi Arabia.

On 10 October 1985, VF-74 and VF-103 F-14As (*Saratoga*/CVW-17), conducted a night, lights-out, interception of an EgyptAir Boeing 737. It was carrying the Palestine Liberation Front terrorists who had killed an American citizen during the hijacking of the Italian cruise liner *Achille Lauro*. CVW-17 F-14As had established several BARCAPs in the Mediterranean, before locating the 737 south of Crete. VAW-125 E-2Cs co-ordinated the operation; VA-85 KA-6Ds, VAQ-137 EA-6Bs, a VQ-2

A HM-14 'Vanguard' RH-53D is offloaded from a USAF C-5A Galaxy at NAVSTA Rota, Spain, in August 1984, ready to participate in Operation *Intense Look*. (NARA)

The scene aboard the Austin-class amphibious transport dock USS *Shreveport* (LPD-12) during Operation *Intense Look*. A HC-4 CH-53E approaches, while three RH-53Ds are seen on deck with their rotors folded. The centre RH-53D displays the 'DH' identification code of HM-12, while the other two display HM-14's 'BJ' code; however, all were operated by the latter squadron, the HM-12 aircraft being borrowed by HM-14. An SH-2F is just visible on *Shreveport's* deck to port. (NARA)

RH-53D BuNo 158748/'531' aboard *Shreveport* during Operation *Intense Look*. This was the aircraft borrowed from HM-12, as seen in the previous image; it had received 'HM-14' titles on the rear fuselage from the outset, but initially retained HM-12's 'DH' code, as seen previously. By the time of this photograph, however, the 'DH' code had been painted over. (NARA)

EA-3B and USAF EC/RC-135s provided support. An E-2C transmitted an order to the EgyptAir crew to divert to Sigonella, Italy; they only complied with this after the E-2C ordered the F-14s to turn on their navigation lights, revealing to the EgyptAir crew that they were surrounded by F-14s! At Sigonella an armed stand-off between U.S. and Italian personnel over jurisdiction was eventually resolved, with Italy taking responsibility for the hijackers.

Libya was suspected of involvement with terrorist outrages including the 27 December 1985 Rome and Vienna airport attacks; U.S.-Libyan relations further deteriorated. *Saratoga*/CVW-17, already in the region, was reinforced by *Coral Sea*/CVW-13 from October 1985, creating Task Force 60 (TF-60). FON Operations *Attain Document I* and *II*, 26–30 January and 12–15 February 1986 respectively, saw F-14As and F/A-18As maintaining CAPs, while A-6Es, A-7Es and F/A-18As conducted Surface CAPs (SUCAPs) searching for Libyan warships. LARAF aircraft were regularly intercepted without incident.

Two red shirt aviation ordnancemen move Mk 20 Rockeye II CBUs across the flight deck of USS *Coral Sea* on 29 January 1986, during Operation *Attain Document I* off Libya. The Rockeye II contained 247 Mk 118 bomblets. Intruders and a Hornet of CVW-13 are seen in the background. This was during *Coral Sea's* first deployment since transferring to LANTFLT, and CVW-13's first sea deployment since being established on 1 March 1984. This Mediterranean deployment took place from October 1985 to May 1986. (NARA)

A VFA-132 'Privateers' F/A-18A is inspected by red shirt aviation ordnancemen during flight operations off Libya aboard *Coral Sea*, also during Operation *Attain Document I* on 29 January 1986. The aircraft is armed with a live AGM-88A HARM. (NARA)

On 19 March TF-60's *Saratoga* and *Coral Sea* CVBGs were joined by the *America* CVBG (CVW-1 embarked), creating TF Zulu. *Attain Document III* commenced on 23 March; TF Zulu's three carriers rotationally covered approximately sixteen hours of flight operations during each forty-eight-hour period. *America* covered 1200–0345 hours, *Coral Sea* 0345–2015 hours and *Saratoga* 2015–1200 hours. They maintained at least twelve CAP aircraft, eight SUCAP aircraft, four S-3As, two E-2Cs, two EA-6Bs and two SH-3Hs continuously airborne. Initially the presence of three CVBGs caused the LARAF to withdraw and disperse many of its fighters into the Libyan interior. When a USN surface action group (SAG) of three cruisers and destroyers crossed the 'Line of Death' at noon on 24 March, covered by the CAP and SUCAP aircraft, the LARAF finally responded, scrambling MiG-25PDs, which were soon engaged by VF-33/CVW-1/*America* F-14As. Permission was eventually granted for the F-14As to open fire, but by then the engagement was over and the MiG-25PDs had withdrawn. Relieving VF-102/CVW-1 F-14As were unsuccessfully attacked by an SA-5 SAM launched from Syrte, resulting in authorisation for USN forces to engage threatening Libyan forces, initiating Operation *Prairie Fire*. As darkness fell, an initial strike by two A-7Es against the Syrte SA-5 site was aborted when an SA-5 engaged them. Soon an E-2C detected a Libyan fast attack craft approaching the SAG; two A-6E SUCAP pairs (two AGM-84A Harpoon-equipped VA-34/CVW-1/*America* A-6Es and two Mk 20 Rockeye II CBU-armed VA-85/CVW-17/Saratoga A-6Es) were vectored in to destroy it. Four CVW-17 A-7Es then returned to the SA-5 site, two VA-81 jets flying high to encourage the site's fire control radar to lock on, allowing two low-flying VA-83 A-7Es to fire two HARMs (its first operational use), one missing, the other destroying the site's 'Square Pair' radar. Two SUCAP VA-85 A-6Es then damaged a Libyan Corvette with Rockeyes; two more approaching with Harpoons aborted as the crippled corvette approached a merchant vessel for assistance. The Syrte SA-5 site was soon repaired, so four VA-83 A-7Es re-attacked the site in a similar fashion to the earlier strike; two HARMs knocked out the two 'Square Pair' radars present. The final act of *Prairie Fire* came at around 0600 on 25 March when a VA-55/CVW-13/*Coral Sea* A-6E attacked another Libyan corvette with APAMs, causing minimal damage. Two VA-85 A-6Es fired a single Harpoon, crippling the corvette; other VA-85 jets finished it off with CBUs. Throughout, VP-56 P-3Cs hunted for any Libyan submarines. USN forces continued to operate in the area without incident until *Attain Document III* was terminated on 27 March.

The following month, despite Libya's increasing isolation, terrorist attacks linked to Libya continued, victims including U.S. citizens. President Reagan ordered pre-planned retaliatory strikes, under Operation *El Dorado Canyon*. While UK-based USAF F-111Fs hit targets around Tripoli to the west (see this author's *USAFE in the 1980s* for details), USN aircraft from *America*/CVW-1 and *Coral Sea*/CVW-13 (*Saratoga* having withdrawn on 30 March) hit targets around Benghazi to the east: the Jamahiriya Guard Barracks and Benina AB, which housed LARAF MiG-23s. Unlike the disastrous 1983 daylight strikes over Lebanon, these attacks would be at night. Prior to the strikes *America* and *Coral Sea* made high-profile visits to north-western Mediterranean ports for the benefit of Libyan attention. Then on the morning of 14 April 1986 they made high-speed, zero electronic-emission, transits back to positions off Libya, evading Soviet ships and Libyan attention, maintaining surprise.

Around midnight on 14/15 April two pairs of VF-33 and VF-102 F-14As (CVW-1/*America*) met the large USAF F-111F/EF-111A/KC-10A formation approaching from the west to escort them; their first act was to ward off Italian F-104S interceptors

A VA-55 'Warhorses' A-6E TRAM (the CO's aircraft, BuNo 159317/'AK-501') recovers aboard *Coral Sea* during operations off Libya on 22 March 1986, the day prior to the commencement of Operation *Attain Document III*. This A-6E carries a live SUCAP load, from the port side: a self-defence AIM-9 on station one, an AGM-84 on station two, an external fuel tank on station three (centreline), an MER with two Mk 20 Rockeye IIs on station four and an empty MER on station five. Heavier loads could be accommodated, but if further unused ordnance was carried it would have to be jettisoned before landing, in order to get down to recovery weight. This was VA-55's first operational deployment since establishment on 7 October 1983. (NARA)

investigating the package. Also around midnight *America* launched six *Iron Hand* VA-46 A-7Es (two carrying four AGM-45s each, four carrying four HARMs each), a VMAQ-2 Det Y EA-6B and a VQ-2 EA-3B to support the western USAF strikes; two each KA-6D and A-7E tankers supported this USN package. Then *America* and *Coral Sea* launched their own Benghazi strike packages. *America* launched six VA-34 A-6Es (two more aborted), two *Iron Hand* VA-72 A-7Es and three VMAQ-2 Det Y EA-6Bs; *Coral Sea* launched eight VA-55 A-6Es and two KA-6Ds, twelve *Iron Hand* F/A-18As (six each from VFA-132 and VMFA-323) and two VAQ-135 EA-6Bs. Two VA-55 A-6Es aborted with malfunctions. Both carriers also provided CAP F-14As and F/A-18As, control E-2Cs, EW EA-3Bs and SAR SH-3Hs.

To the west, ahead of the F-111s, four of the six *Iron Hand* VA-46 A-7Es launched their sixteen HARMs at Libyan radars as they switched on in response to the incoming raid. Surviving sites were engaged closer-in by the eight AGM-45s of the two remaining A-7Es.

To the east, the six remaining VA-55 A-6Es, one armed with Mk 82SE (Snake Eye) 500 lb retarded bombs, five with APAMs, looped behind Benina AB to attack it from the south. Two VAQ-135 EA-6Bs, and one from VMAQ-2 Det Y, trailed behind the A-6Es, jamming Libyan defences. Meanwhile VFA-132 F/A-18As, approaching from the north, fired HARMs at Libyan radars. At 0200 hours local time the A-6Es accurately dropped twelve Mk 82SEs and sixty APAMs over Benina, cratering the runway and destroying at least three MiG-23MS, two Mi-8 helicopters, one G.222 transport, one Boeing 727 airliner and one SF.260 trainer. Further aircraft and buildings were damaged.

Meanwhile, to the north-west of Benina, VA-34's six A-6Es, with six VMFA-323 F/A-18As, two VA-72 A-7Es and one VAQ-135 EA-6B hit Benghazi's Jamahiriya Guard Barracks. SAM-sites were engaged by F/A-18As with HARMs and A-7Es with AGM-45s;

Bomb skids loaded with CBU-59 APAMs on *Coral Sea's* flight deck, prior to being loaded aboard VA-55 A-6Es on 15 April 1986 ahead of Operation *El Dorado Canyon*. These CBU-59 APAMs were destined to be dropped on Benina AB. Although the CBU-59 APAM used the same Mk 7 cluster bomb dispenser body as the earlier Mk 20 Rockeye II, the CBU-59 carried 717 smaller BLU-77/B bomblets with improved anti-personnel/anti-material effectiveness. The black lightning bolt painted on the munition visually differentiated APAM from a Rockeye II. A VA-55 A-6E TRAM and KA-6D are behind, with F/A-18As in the background. (NARA)

EA-6B jammed radars. The A-6Es each dropped twelve Mk 82SEs over the target, destroying the barracks, a MiG-23 assembly building and several MiG-23 airframes in shipping crates. Two bombs fell wide of their targets, landing in civilian areas.

Operation *El Dorado Canyon* was the start of a more concerted U.S. response to terrorism, with Libya becoming increasingly isolated.

While the Sixth Fleet remained preoccupied with Libya, during the 1980s most carriers (both LANTFLT and PACFLT) operating within the Seventh Fleet AOR spent time in the Indian Ocean monitoring Iran.

The Persian Gulf 'Tanker War' phase of the Iran-Iraq war commenced when Iraq targeted an Iranian oil terminal and oil tankers. Iran soon responded by targeting Kuwaiti tankers that were transporting Iraqi crude oil, later expanding attacks to tankers of other Gulf states supporting Iraq. Consequently, Kuwaiti tankers were re-flagged as U.S. ships, allowing them to be escorted in convoys by USN warships from July 1987 under Operation *Earnest Will*. When these convoys immediately encountered sea mines, MCM forces were rushed to the region, including eight HM-14 RH-53Ds embarked aboard USS *Guadalcanal* (LPH-7), which also carried HMM-263(-)(REINFORCED) with its usual CH-46Es reinforced with AH-1Ts and

A green shirt Air Wing Maintenance crewman checks the VA-72 CO's A-7E (BuNo 160549/'AB-401') aboard USS *America* during flight operations off Libya on 17 April 1986. It is armed with an *Iron Hand* loadout: an AGM-45 is visible on station one, a Mk 20 Rockeye II on station two, an external tank on station three and an AIM-9L on station four (the cheek hardpoint). All ordnance is live. *America* and CVW-1 were at the start of a March to September 1986 Mediterranean deployment, hence the still tidy appearance of this A-7E's TPS camouflage. (NARA)

Aviation ordnancemen load an AIM-9L onto an AH-1T SeaCobra attached to HMM-263(-)(REINFORCED) aboard the Iwo Jima-class amphibious assault ship USS *Guadalcanal* (LPH-7), on 18 August 1987 in the Persian Gulf during Operation *Earnest Will*. AH-1Ts escorted the RH-53Ds while they undertook their MCM duties. (NARA)

An HM-14 RH-53D tows its minesweeping sled (out of shot) on 1 October 1987, during *Earnest Will* MCM operations in the Persian Gulf. (NARA)

UH-1Ns. The convoys were monitored by USN P-3Cs deployed to Dhahran, Saudi Arabia; these were in turn protected by VF-21/VF-154 F-14As of *Constellation*/ CVW-14 on Gonzo Station in the Gulf of Oman. On 8 August 1987 a VAW-113 E-2C from *Constellation* detected an Islamic Republic of Iran Air Force (IRIAF), 91st TFS, F-4E heading west, low over the sea, attempting to intercept a USN P-3C. The F-4E ignored the E-2C's warnings and continued towards the P-3C, so the latter was ordered to head south, away from the threat, while two VF-21 F-14As on CAP at 20,000 feet were ordered to engage the F-4E. The Iranian jet had been under ground radar control, but now within 20 miles of the P-3C, it climbed to 2,000 feet and powered-up its APQ-120 radar; seconds later it fired an AIM-7E-2 Sparrow at the P-3C. The F-14As quickly responded. The number two F-14A launched an AIM-7F at a range of 16 km (8.6 nm), but its engine failed to ignite and it fell away. The lead F-14A fired an AIM-7M within 15 km (7.5 nm) and the number two fired another AIM-7F, both launched at the limits of their envelopes. However, the IRIAF F-4E crew, alerted by their radar warning receiver (RWR) that the F-14As had fired upon them, were forced to brake away hard and down to the sea surface, therefore breaking radar lock with the P-3C and causing their AIM-7E to stop homing on its target. The number two F-14A's AIM-7F detonated near the IRIAF F-4E as it tried to escape, damaging its fin, but it managed to return to its base at Bandar Abbas.

Also during the tanker war, a modified Iraqi Dassault Falcon 50 fired two Exocet anti-ship missiles at the frigate USS *Stark* (FFG-31) on 17 May 1987, leaving thirty-six sailors dead, one missing, and twenty-one wounded; Iraq claimed that the attack

The HC-2 Det 2 'Desert Duck' SH-3G taking off on 1 January 1989 from Mobile Sea Base *Hercules*, a leased barge positioned in the Persian Gulf and manned by east coast naval special warfare units during Operation *Prime Chance*. This was an August 1987 to June 1989 United States Special Operations Command operation to protect U.S.-flagged oil tankers from Iranian attack; it ran in parallel to the July 1987 to September 1988 Operation *Earnest Will*. (NARA)

resulted from mistaken identity. HC-2 Det 2's SH-3G flew flight surgeon lieutenant commander Terry A. Miller and supplies to the *Stark* from NSA Bahrain, subsequently conducting an unsuccessful search for survivors in the water.

Ongoing Iranian mining of the Persian Gulf culminated in the frigate USS *Samuel B. Roberts* (FFG-58) striking an Iranian mine on 14 April 1988, causing considerable damage but fortunately no loss of life. The response was Operation *Praying Mantis*, launched on 18 April, with USN surface units committed to action alongside CVW-11's air units embarked aboard *Enterprise* in the Indian Ocean. Marine Air-Ground Task Force (MAGTF) 2–88, aboard USS *Trenton* (LPD-14), which included an air element provided by HMLA-167(-)(REINFORCED), with four AH-1Ts, two UH-1Ns and two CH-46Es, was also committed.

At sunrise, U.S. warships and MAGTF 2–88 seized oil platforms used by Iranian forces for surveillance and to launch attacks. After the Iranians ignored radio messages to evacuate and opened fire at U.S. forces, AH-1Ts engaged the platforms with TOW missiles and their guns; UH-1Ns and CH-46Es then delivered Marines to assault the platforms. During the operation one AH-1T crashed with the loss of its two crew. Warship-based SH-2Fs and SH-60Bs supported the operation. Meanwhile, surface units engaged Iranian fast attack craft *Joshan*, and CVW-11 launched A-6Es (VA-95) and A-7Es (VA-22/VA-94) into the gulf, hunting for Iranian warships; a primary 'War at Sea' package of two A-6Es and six A-7Es (three from each squadron) and other A-6Es/A-7Es on SUCAPs. VF-114/VF-213 F-14As provided CAP. E-2Cs (VAW-117), EA-6Bs (VAQ-135) and other types supported, as did P-3Cs (VP-46) flying from NSA Bahrain. An E-2C detected *Boghammar* speed boats attacking various maritime targets, which A-6Es attacked with Rockeyes. Later in the day more Iranian naval units were getting underway. When an

A-6E performed a low pass of the Iranian frigate *Sahand*, it was believed by the A-6E crew to have opened fire on them. Their ROE satisfied, they climbed away and returned to dive-bomb *Sahand* with a 500 lb GBU-12 laser guided bomb (LGB), which narrowly missed but probably caused hull damage; they reattacked with a Harpoon from 15 miles, which struck amidships, then fired their two AGM-123 Skipper II missiles (which combined a GBU-16 1,000 lb LGB with a former AGM-45 rocket motor, increasing its stand-off range), one of which hit near *Sahand's* bridge. USS *Joseph Strauss* (DDG-16) also fired a Harpoon at *Sahand*. The six 'War at Sea' package A-7Es delivered the *coup de grâce* with their mixed ordnance; the lead pair were armed with AGM-62 Walleye IIs and Mk 83 1,000 lb dumb bombs, the second pair with Mk 83s and datalink pods to guide the lead pair's Walleyes, and the final pair with Mk 83s. *Sahand's* sister ship *Sabalan* was noted putting to sea from Bandar Abbas; an A-6E attacked her with a GBU-12 LGB, which left *Sabalan* dead in the water; other CVW-11 aircraft were inbound to sink *Sabalan*, but the 'knock it off' order arrived before they could do so. Operation *Praying Mantis* was the largest U.S. surface engagement since the Second World War.

The decade closed as it began, seeing another clash with Libyan fighters. U.S.-Libyan tensions were rising again by 1989, when *John F. Kennedy*/CVW-3 was in the Mediterranean. On 4 January 1989 VA-75 A-6Es were exercising south of Crete, around 130 km north of Libya. Two F-14A CAP pairs (a VF-14 pair to the west, VF-32 pair to the east), controlled by a VAW-126 E-2C, protected them. New ROE allowed the USN to engage the Libyans if they merely approached in a 'threatening fashion', even if the Libyans did not fire first, as the LARAF now operated more medium-range AAM-equipped fighters. The VF-32 pair, Gypsy 207 BuNo 159610/'AC-207' (pilot Commander Joseph B. Connelly, RIO Commander Leo F. Enwright) and Gypsy 202 BuNo 159437/'AC-202' (pilot Lieutenant Hermon C. Cook III, RIO Lieutenant Commander Stephen Patrick Collins) were alerted that LARAF MiG-23MFs had scrambled. The F-14As turned south-east towards the MiG-23MFs, acquiring them on their AWG-9 radars at 115 km (72 miles). Normally, being 'painted' by F-14 radars resulted in LARAF fighters turning away. However, as the F-14s then turned away to the south-west, the MiG-23s turned abruptly north towards the F-14As, while climbing and accelerating. The F-14s made several heading changes; each time the MiG-23s changed their heading back towards the F-14s. Now on a collision course, the F-14s heading south and the MiGs heading north, closing at 1,852 km/h (1,000 knots) the F-14s were authorised to open fire in self-defence. When 19 km away Enwright in Gypsy 207 launched two AIM-7s at the lead MiG. Neither hit the target. The F-14s split, Gypsy 207 hard right, Gypsy 202 hard left. The MiGs swung toward Cook in Gypsy 202, who reversed his turn to face the MiGs again, then fired a head-on AIM-7 at 9.6 km, destroying the one MiG in a fireball. As Cook avoided his victim's debris, Connelly came up behind the other MiG. After briefly struggling to get an AIM-9 lock-on tone, he did so and launched, destroying the other MiG. Both MiG pilots were seen to eject. The F-14s, not hanging around for another MiG-23 pair that had since scrambled, dropped to low level and accelerated back north.

The December 1989 coup attempt against Philippine President Aquino resulted in U.S. airpower intervening; Operation *Classic Resolve* saw *Midway*/CVW-5 and *Enterprise*/CVW-11 conduct flight operations in the area until the situation subsided. E-2Cs of VAW-115 (CVW-5) and VAW-117 (CVW-11) provided continuous radar coverage of the Manila Bay area, supporting USAF F-4s flying from Clark AB to deter Filipino aircraft from taking off and attacking Manila.

Bibliography

Cole, Ronald H., *Operation Urgent Fury* (Washington: Joint History Office, Office of the Chairman of the Joint Chiefs of Staff, 1997)

Cooper, Tom, *In the Claws of the Tomcat* (Warwick: Helion & Company Limited, 2021)

Cooper, Tom, Delalande, Arnaud, and Grandolini, Albert, *Libyan Air Wars Parts 1, 2 and 3* (Solihull: Helion & Company Limited, 2014/16)

Donald, David (Ed.), *US Navy & Marine Corps Air Power Directory* (London: Aerospace Publishing Limited, 1992)

Donald, David and Marsh, Daniel J., *Carrier Aviation Air Power Directory* (Norwalk: AIRtime Publishing Inc., 2001)

Donald, David, and Lake, Jon (Eds.), *Encyclopedia of World Military Aircraft Volumes 1 & 2* (London: Aerospace Publishing Limited, 1994)

Elward, Brad, *Nimitz-Class Aircraft Carriers* (Oxford: Osprey Publishing, 2010)

Elward, Brad, *US Cold War Aircraft Carriers* (Oxford: Osprey Publishing, 2014)

Evans, Mark L., and Grossnick, Roy A., *United States Naval Aviation 1910–2010 Volumes I and II* (Washington, D.C.: Naval History and Heritage Command, Department of the Navy, 2015)

Grossnick, Roy A., *United States Naval Aviation 1910–1995* (Washington D.C.: Naval Historical Center, Department of the Navy, 1997)

Hopkins III, Robert S., *The Boeing KC-135 Stratotanker: More Than a Tanker* (Manchester: Crécy Publishing Limited, 2018)

Lake, Jon (Ed.), *McDonnell F-4 Phantom Spirit in the Sky* (London: Aerospace Publishing Limited, 1992)

Morgan, Rick, *A-6 Intruder Units 1974–96* (Oxford: Osprey Publishing, 2017)

Mersky, Peter, with Crutch, Mike, and Holmes, Tony, *A-7 Corsair II Units 1975–91* (Oxford: Osprey Publishing, 2021)

Romano, Angelo, and Herndon, John D., *From Bats to Rangers* (Simi Valley: Ginter Books, 2017)

Romano, Angelo, *Electronic Aggressors Part One* (Simi Valley: Ginter Books, 2019)

Romano, Angelo, *Electronic Aggressors Part Two* (Simi Valley: Ginter Books, 2019)

Romano, Angelo, *World Watchers* (Simi Valley: Ginter Books, 2020)

Symonds, Adrian, *TAC in the 1980s* (Stroud: Amberley Publishing, 2021)

Symonds, Adrian, *USAFE in the 1980s* (Stroud: Amberley Publishing, 2020)

Williamson, Justin W., *Operation Eagle Claw 1980* (Oxford: Osprey Publishing, 2020)

Yenne, Bill, *US Cruise Missiles* (Forest Lake: Specialty Press, 2018)

Journals and Periodicals:

World Air Power Journal, various volumes (Aerospace Publishing Limited)

Unpublished Papers:

OPNAV Notice C5400: Promulgation of Naval Aeronautical Organization (April 1980 through October 1989 publications)

Appendix I

Carrier Air Wings 1980

Atlantic Fleet

CVW-1 (AB) – USS *John F. Kennedy* (CV-67)

VF-14 – F-14A (100)
VF-32 – F-14A (200)
VA-46 – A-7E (300)
VA-72 – A-7E (400)
VA-34 – A-6E/KA-6D (500)
VAQ-138 – EA-6B (610)
VS-32 – S-3A (700)
HS-11 – SH-3H (730)
VAW-126 – E-2C (010)

CVW-1 conducted a Mediterranean cruise 4 August 1980–28 March 1981. A VQ-2 Det (EA-3B – retaining JQ identification letters) joined CVW-1 for the cruise. Following that cruise, CVW-1 was reorganised and reassigned to USS *America* (CV 66) prior to its next cruise in 1982.

CVW-3 (AC) – USS *Saratoga* (CV-60)

VF-31 – F-4J (100)
VF-103 – F-4J (200)
VA-37 – A-7E (300)
VA-105 – A-7E (400)
VA-75 – A-6E/KA-6D (500)
VS-22 – S-3A (700)
HS-7 – SH-3H (730)
VAW-123 – E-2C (010)

CVW-3 conducted a Mediterranean cruise 10 March–27 August 1980.

CVW-6 (AE) – USS *Independence* (CV-62)

VF-102 – F-4J (100)
VF-33 – F-4J (200)
VA-15 – A-7E (300)

VA-87 – A-7E (400)
VA-176 – A-6E/KA-6D (500)
VAW-122 – E-2C (600–603)
VAQ-131 – EA-6B (604–607)
HS-15 – SH-3H (610–615)
VS-28 – S-3A (700)

CVW-6 conducted a Mediterranean/ Indian Ocean cruise 19 November 1980–10 June 1981; VFP-63 Det.4 (RF-8G 616–620) joined CVW-6 for the deployment.

CVW-7 (AG) – USS *Dwight D. Eisenhower* (CVN-69)

VF-143 – F-14A (100)
VF-142 – F-14A (200)
VA-66 – A-7E (300)
VA-12 – A-7E (400)
VA-65 – A-6E/KA-6D (500)
VAQ-132 – EA-6B (610)
VAW-121 – E-2C (010)
VS-31 – S-3A/US-3A (700)
HS-5 – SH-3H (730)

CVW-7 conducted a Mediterranean/ Indian Ocean cruise 15 April–22 December 1980, joined by a VQ-2 Det (EA-3B – JQ) and a HM-14 Det (RH-53D – BJ).

CVW-8 (AJ) – USS *Nimitz* (CVN-68)

VF-41 – F-14A (100)
VF-84 – F-14A (200)
VA-82 – A-7E (300)
VA-86 – A-7E (400)
VA-35 – A-6E/KA-6D (500)
VFP-63 Det 5 – RF-8G (600)
VAQ-134 – EA-6B (610)

VS-24 – S-3A (700)
HS-9 – SH-3H (730)
VAW-112 – E-2B (010)

CVW-8 conducted a Mediterranean/ Indian Ocean/Arabian Sea cruise (including Iran hostage rescue operations) 10 September 1979–26 May 1980, joined by a HM-16 Det (RH-53D – GC) between November 1979 and 19 May 1980, as well as VQ-1 Det B (EA-3B – PR) and a VRC-50 Det (C-2A – RG) both attached January–April 1980.

CVW-8/*Nimitz* conducted a further cruise 29 August–17 October 1980 to the North Atlantic (NORLANT) to participate in Exercise Teamwork '80, deploying without VFP-63 Det 5 or VAQ-134 and with VAW-124 (E-2C – 010) in lieu of VAW-112.

CVW-17 (AA) – USS *Forrestal* (CV-59)

VF-11 – F-4J (100)
VF-74 – F-4J (200)
VA-83 – A-7E (300)
VA-81 – A-7E (400)
VA-85 – A-6E/KA-6D (500)
VFP-63 Det. – RF-8G (600)
VAQ-133 – EA-6B (610)
VS-30 – S-3A (700)
HS-3 – SH-3D/H (730)
VAW-125 – E-2C (010)

CVW-17 conducted a Mediterranean cruise 27 November 1979–7 May 1980.

CVWR-20 (AF) – Naval Air Reserve

VF-201 – F-4N (100)
VF-202 – F-4N (200)
VA-203 – A-7B (300)
VA-204 – A-7B (400)
VA-205 – A-7B (500)
VFP-206 – RF-8G (600)
VAK-208 – KA-3B (610)
VAQ-209 – EA-6A (700)
VAW-78 – E-2B (010)
HS-84 – SH-3D (NW 400)

Pacific Fleet

CVW-2 (NE) – USS *Ranger* (CV-61)

VF-1 – F-14A (100)
VF-2 – F-14A (200)
VA-113 – A-7E (300)
VA-25 – A-7E (400)
VA-145 – A-6E/KA-6D (500)
VAW-117 – E-2B (600)
VAQ-137 – EA-6B (620)
VS-37 – S-3A (700)
HS-2 – SH-3H (720)

CVW-2 conducted a West Pacific (WESTPAC) and Indian Ocean cruise 10 September 1980–5 May 1981. A VQ-1 Det (EA-3B – retaining PR identification letters) joined CVW-2 for the deployment.

CVW-5 (NF) - USS *Midway* (CV-41)

VF-161 – F-4J (100)
VF-151 – F-4J (200)
VA-93 – A-7E (300)
VA-56 – A-7E (400)
VA-115 – A-6E/KA-6D (500)
VAW-115 – E-2B (601-604)
VMFP-3 Det – RF-4B (RF 610)
VMAQ-2 Det – EA-6B (CY 620)
HC-1 Det.2 – SH-3G (722-727)

CVW-5 conducted WESTPAC/Indian Ocean cruises 30 September 1979–20 February 1980, and 14 July–26 November 1980. Following the latter VF-151/161 transitioned from F-4J to F-4S between December 1980 and February 1981 and VAQ-136 replaced the VMAQ-2 Det. VA-115 also transitioned from A-6E/ KA-6D to A-6E TRAM/KA-6D, receiving five A-6E TRAMs at Atsugi on 10 May 1980, and five more during 1981.

CVW-9 (NG) – USS *Constellation* (CV-64)

VF-211 – F-14A (100)
VF-24 – F-14A (200)
VA-146 – A-7E (300)

VA-147 – A-7E (400)
VA-165 – A-6E/KA-6D (500)
VAW-116 – E-2C (600)
VFP-63 Det.3 – RF-8G (610)
VS-38 – S-3A (700)
HS-6 – SH-3H (720)

CVW-9 conducted a WESTPAC/Indian Ocean cruise (including participation in Exercise RIMPAC '80) 26 February–15 October 1980, joined by a VQ-1 Det (EA-3B – PR)

CVW-11 (NH) – USS *America* (CV-66)

VF-114 – F-14A (100)
VF-213 – F-14A (200)
VA-192 – A-7E (300)
VA-195 – A-7E (400)
VA-95 – A-6E/KA-6D (500)
VAW-124 – E-2C (600–603)
VFP-63 Det 4 – RF-8G (615–617)
VAQ-131 – EA-6B (620–623)
VS-33 – S-3A (700)
HS-12 - SH-3H (740–745)

The above organisation was during CVW-11's 13 March–22 September 1979 Mediterranean cruise; CVW-11 did not deploy again until a Mediterranean/Indian Ocean cruise 14 April–12 November 1981, during which VAW-123 (E-2C – 600-603) replaced VAW-124, VAQ-133 (EA-6B – 604–607) replaced VAQ-131, VS-33 added a US-3A to its S-3As and no VFP-63 Det was included. The 1981 cruise also included VQ-2 Det A (EA-3B – JQ) and VR-24 Det A (C-2A – JM) while HS-12 adopted 610 series MODEX numbers for its SH-3Hs.

CVW-14 (NK) – USS *Coral Sea* (CV-43)

VMFA-323 – F-4N (100)
VMFA-531 – F-4N (200)
VA-97 – A-7E (300)
VA-27 – A-7E (400)
VA-196 – A-6E/KA-6D (500)
VAW-113 – E-2B (600)

VFP-63 Det.2 – RF-8G (610)
HC-1 Det.3 – SH-3G (720)

CVW-14 conducted a WESTPAC/Indian Ocean cruise with the above 13 November 1979–11 June 1980, following which CVW-14 was reorganised prior to its next cruise in 1981: VF-154/VF-21 (F-4N – 100/200) replaced VMFA-323/VMFA-531, while VFP-63 Det.2's RF-8Gs switched to 115–117 MODEX numbers. CVW-14/*Coral Sea* briefly deployed to the Hawaii Operating Area 4 May–6 June 1981, adding a VRC-30 Det (C-1A - RW) for this. CVW-14 then joined *Coral Sea* for her final WESTPAC/Indian Ocean cruise (prior to reassignment to the Atlantic Fleet) 20 August 1981–23 March 1982 (HC-1 Det.3 switching to 610 MODEX numbers for this cruise).

CVW-15 (NL) – USS *Kitty Hawk* (CV-63)

VF-51 – F-14A (100)
VF-111 – F-14A (200)
VA-22 – A-7E (300)
VA-94 – A-7E (400)
VA-52 – A-6E/KA-6D (500)
VAW-114 – E-2C (600)
VFP-63 Det.1 – RF-8G (610)
VAQ-135 – EA-6B (624–627)
VS-21 – S-3A/US-3A (700)
HS-8 – SH-3H (720)

CVW-15 conducted a WESTPAC cruise 30 May 1979–25 February 1980, a VQ-1 Det (EA-3B – PR) joining CVW-15 for this.

CVWR-30 (ND) – Naval Air Reserve

VF-301 – F-4N (100)
VF-302 – F-4N (200)
VA-303 – A-7B (300)
VA-304 – A-7B (400)
VA-305 – A-7B (500)
VFP-306 – RF-8G (600)
VAQ-309 – EA-6A (610)
VAW-88 – E-2B (010)
VAK-308 – KA-3B (630)
HS-85 – SH-3D (NW 610)

Appendix II

Carrier Air Wings 1989

Atlantic Fleet

CVW-1 (AB) – USS *America* (CV-66)

VF-102 – F-14A (100)
VF-33 – F-14A (200)
VFA-82 – F/A-18C (300)
VFA-86 – F/A-18C (400)
VA-85 – A-6E/KA-6D (500)
VAW-123 – E-2C (600–603)
VAQ-137 – EA-6B (604–607)
HS-11 – SH-3H (610)
VS-32 – S-3A (700)

CVW-1 conducted two cruises aboard USS *America* during 1989: 8 February–3 April (North Atlantic) and 11 May–10 November (Mediterranean/Indian Ocean).

CVW-3 (AC) – USS *John F. Kennedy* (CV-67)

VF-14 – F-14A (100)
VF-32 – F-14A (200)
VA-75 – A-6E/KA-6D (500)
VMA(AW)-533 – A-6E (540)
VAW-126 – E-2C (600–603)
VAQ-130 – EA-6B (604–607)
HS-7 – SH-3H (610)
VS-22 – S-3A (700)

CVW-3 conducted a Mediterranean cruise 2 August 1988–1 February 1989.

CVW-6 (AE) – USS *Forrestal* (CV-59)

VF-11 – F-14A (100)
VF-31 – F-14A (200)
VA-37 – A-7E (300)
VA-105 – A-7E (400)

VA-176 – A-6E/KA-6D (500)
VAW-122 – E-2C (600-603)
VAQ-142 – EA-6B (604-607)
HS-15 – SH-3H (610)
VS-28 – S-3A (700)

CVW-6 conducted a Mediterranean cruise 4 November 1989–12 April 1990. For CVW-6's previous cruise on *Forrestal* (Mediterranean/Indian Ocean, 25 April–7 October 1988) VAQ-132 had been the assigned EA-6B squadron.

CVW-7 (AG) – USS *Dwight D. Eisenhower* (CVN-69)

VF-143 – F-14A+ (100)
VF-142 – F-14A+ (200)
VFA-136 – F/A-18A (300)
VFA-131 – F/A-18A (400)
VA-34 – A-6E/KA-6D (500)
VAW-121 – E-2C (600–603)
VAQ-140 – EA-6B (604–607)
HS-5 – SH-3H (610)
VS-31 – S-3B (700)

CVW-7 conducted cruises 17 April–20 May 1989 (for Joint Exercise Solid Shield '89 off the South Carolina coast) and 6 October–2 November 1989 (off the North Carolina coast).

CVW-8 (AJ) – USS *Theodore Roosevelt* (CVN-71)

VF-41 – F-14A (100)
VF-84 – F-14A (200)
VFA-15 – F/A-18A (300)
VFA-87 – F/A-18A (400)
VA-35 – A-6E (500)
VA-36 – A-6E (530)

VAW-124 – E-2C (600)
HS-9 – SH-3H (610)
VAQ-141 – EA-6B (620)
VS-24 – S-3A (700)

CVW-8 conducted a North Atlantic cruise 30 December 1988–30 June 1989

CVW-13 (AK) – USS *Coral Sea* (CV-43)

VMFA-451 – F/A-18A (100)
VFA-132 – F/A-18A (200)
VFA-137 – F/A-18A (300)
VA-55 – A-6E (500)
VA-65 – A-6E/KA-6D (510)
VAW-127 – E-2C (600–603)
VAQ-133 – EA-6B (604–607)
HS-17 – SH-3H (610)

CVW-13 conducted a Mediterranean cruise 31 May–3 September 1989.

CVW-17 (AA) – USS *Saratoga* (CV-60)

CVW-17 had been assigned to USS *Saratoga* (CV-60) since USS *Forrestal* (CV-59) entered a three-year Service Life Extension Program (SLEP) in November 1982. The composition of CVW-17 for its final 1980s cruise with *Saratoga* (5 June–16 November 1987 – Mediterranean) was:

VF-74 – F-14A (100)
VF-103 – F-14A (200)
VA-83 – A-7E (300)
VA-81 – A-7E (400)
VA-85 – A-6E/KA-6D (500)
VAW-125 – E-2C (600–603)
VAQ-137 – EA-6B (604–607)
HS-3 – SH-3H (610)
VS-30 – S-3A (700)
VQ-2 Det – EA-3B (JQ)

However, CVW-17s final cruise of the 1980s was with USS *Independence* (CV-62), which was conducting a homeport change (Norfolk to San Diego, 15 August–8 October 1988) as it transferred from the Atlantic Fleet to the Pacific Fleet. CVW-17's non-standard composition for this cruise was:

VFA-131 – F/A-18A (AK 100)
VF-103 – F-14A (200)
VA-155 – A-6E (500)
VA-85 Det – A-6E/KA-6D (AB 520)
VAW-125 – E-2C (600)
HS-3 – SH-3H (610)
VS-30 – S-3A (700)
VRC-30 Det.62 – C-2A (RW)

CVW-17 remained assigned to *Saratoga* after its brief association with *Independence*, however CVW-17 did not conduct another cruise with *Saratoga* until August 1990 (for Operations Desert Shield/Storm).

CVWR-20 (AF) – Naval Air Reserve

VF-201 – F-14A (100)
VF-202 – F-14A (200)
VA-203 – A-7E (300)
VA-204 – A-7E (400)
VA-205 – A-7E (500)
VAK-208 – KA-3B (disestablished 30 September 1989)
HS-75 – SH-3D
VAQ-209 – EA-6A
VAW-78 – E-2C

CVWR-20 deployed (except VAK-208) aboard USS *Dwight D. Eisenhower* (CVN-69) to conduct cyclic operations 24 July–3 August 1989 (Western Atlantic – WESTLANT).

Pacific Fleet

CVW-2 (NE) – USS *Ranger* (CV-61)

VF-1 – F-14A (100)
VF-2 – F-14A (200)

VMA(AW)-121 – A-6E (400)
VA-145 – A-6E (500)
VAW-116 – E-2C (600–603)
VAQ-131 – EA-6B (604–607)
HS-14 – SH-3H (610)
VS-38 – S-3A (700)

CVW-2 conducted a WESTPAC/Indian Ocean cruise 24 February–24 August 1989, adding a VRC-50 Det (US-3A – RG)

CVW-5 (NF) – USS *Midway* (CV-41)

VFA-195 – F/A-18A (100)
VFA-151 – F/A-18A (200)
VFA-192 – F/A-18A (300)
VA-185 – A-6E/KA-6D (400)
VA-115 – A-6E/KA-6D (500)
VAW-115 – E-2C (600–603)
VAQ-136 – EA-6B (604–607)
HS-12 – SH-3H (610)

CVW-5 conducted WESTPAC cruises 21 January–24 February 1989, 27 February–9 April 1989 and 31 May–25 July 1989, and a WESTPAC/Indian Ocean cruise 15 August–11 December 1989.

CVW-9 (NG) – USS *Nimitz* (CVN-68)

VF-211 – F-14A (100)
VF-24 – F-14A (200)
VA-146 – A-7E (300)
VA-147 – A-7E (400)
VA-165 – A-6E/KA-6D (500)
VAW-112 – E-2C (600–603)
VAQ-138 – EA-6B (604–607)
HS-2 – SH-3H (610)
VS-33 – S-3A (700)

CVW-9 conducted cruises 2 September 1988–2 March 1989 (WESTPAC/Indian Ocean) and 15 June–9 July 1989 (North Pacific – NORPAC), adding VRC-30 Det.68 (C-2A – RW) for the latter.

CVW-11 (NH) – USS *Enterprise* (CVN-65)

VF-114 – F-14A (100)
VF-213 – F-14A (200)
VA-22 – A-7E (300)
VA-94 – A-7E (400)
VA-95 – A-6E/KA-6D (500)
VAW-117 – E-2C (600–603)
VAQ-135 – EA-6B (604–607)
HS-6 – SH-3H (610)
VS-21 – S-3A (700)

CVW-11 conducted a world cruise (from Alameda to its new homeport at Norfolk, where *Enterprise* would subsequently serve with the Atlantic Fleet) 17 September 1989–16 March 1990.

CVW-14 (NK) – USS *Constellation* (CV-64)

VF-154 – F-14A (100)
VF-21 – F-14A (200)
VFA-113 – F/A-18A (300)
VFA-25 – F/A-18A (400)
VA-196 – A-6E/KA-6D (500)
VAW-113 – E-2C (600–603)
VAQ-139 – EA-6B (604–607)
HS-8 – SH-3H (610)
VS-37 – S-3A (700)

CVW-14 conducted cruises 1 December 1988–1 June 1989 (WESTPAC/Indian Ocean) and 16 September–19 October 1989 (NORPAC), adding VRC-30 Det.64 (C-2A – RW) for the latter.

CVW-15 (NL) – USS *Carl Vinson* (CVN-70)

VF-51 – F-14A (100)
VF-111 – F-14A (200)
VA-97 – A-7E (300)
VA-27 – A-7E (400)
VA-52 – A-6E/KA-6D (500)
VAW-114 – E-2C (600–603)
VAQ-134 – EA-6B (604–607)

HS-4 – SH-3H (610)
VS-29 – S-3A (700)

CVW-15 conducted a NORPAC/WESTPAC cruise 18 September–8 November 1989.

CVWR-30 (ND) – Naval Air Reserve

VF-301 – F-14A (100)
VF-302 – F-14A (200)
VFA-303 – F/A-18A (300)
VA-304 – A-6E/KA-6D (400)
VFA-305 – F/A-18A (500)
VAW-88 – E-2C (600–603)
VAQ-309 – EA-6A (604–607)
HS-85 – SH-3H (NW 610)

Note

CVW-10 (NM)

Not included in the above listing is short-lived CVW-10, established 1 November 1986, but soon disestablished on 30 September 1988. Originally intended to serve with USS *Abraham Lincoln* (CVN-72), its only sea deployment saw elements of CVW-10 conduct carrier qualifications (CARQUALS) aboard USS *Enterprise* (CVN-65) 24 July–5 August 1987 during Exercise BEHAVIOUR CRITERION 87-20 in the EASTPAC. VA-155 was not established until 1 September 1987, therefore it was obviously not involved in this deployment.

It was intended that CVW-10 would embark aboard USS *Independence* (CV-62) for the latter's 1988 Norfolk to San Diego homeport change, and CVW-10 aircraft began to receive 'USS INDEPENDENCE' titles in 1987. However, on 22 January 1988 it was decided to disestablish CVW-10 later in the year, and (as noted above) CVW-17 embarked aboard *Independence* for her homeport change instead.

CVW-10 never received a full complement of squadrons; those which were assigned (all except VA-155 disestablished during 1988) were:

VF-191 – F-14A (100)
VF-194 – F-14A (200)
VFA-161 – F/A-18A (400)
VA-155 – A-6E (500)
VAW-111 – E-2C (600)
HS-16 – SH-3H (610)
VS-35 – S-3A (700)